Apuleius

○ ◑ ◐ ◕ ● ◔ ○ ○

The Metamorphoses
Book 1

Latin Text, Notes, Vocabulary

James S. Ruebel

with a Foreword by
Stephen Nimis

Bolchazy-Carducci Publishers, Inc.
Mundelein, Illinois USA

Editor: Laurie Haight Keenan

Contributing Editor: Georgia Irby-Massie

Cover & Book Design: Cameron A. Marshall

Latin Text: The Latin text based on R. Helm (Teubner, 2d edition, 1913)

Cover Images: Full Moon: NASA–Color Composite of Moon; *Half Moon*: NASA Photo
    Number P-41508C; *Tree Photography*: Cameron A. Marshall

Bolchazy-Carducci Publishers, Inc.
1570 Baskin Road
Mundelein, Illinois 60060
www.bolchazy.com

Printed in the United States of America
2011
by CreateSpace

ISBN 978-0-86516-484-0

Library of Congress Cataloging-in-Publication Data

Apuleius
[Metamorphoses. Book 1]
The metamorphoses. Book 1 / Apuleius ; [compiled by] James S. Ruebel ; with a foreword by Stephen Nimis.
    p. cm.
Includes bibliographical references.
Text in Latin with English commentary, notes, and glossary.
ISBN 0-86516-484-3 (pbk. : alk. paper)
1. Mythology, Classical—Fiction. 2. Metamorphosis—Fiction. I. Ruebel, James S., 1945- II. Title.

PA6207 .M33 2000
873'.01—dc21

00-050803

Contents

○ ◑ ◐ ● ◐ ◑ ○

Acknowledgments

○ ◑ ◕ ● ◐ ◑ ○

This edition has its origin in a Latin class taught at Iowa State University in Fall 1997, where Book 1 was read in advance of the Cupid and Psyche tale. The notes here are much expanded versions of the patched-together classroom aids I distributed to that group. I am grateful to those students for their perceptive questions and enthusiastic participation, which made this book better than it would otherwise have been. I am also grateful to the anonymous reader for Bolchazy-Carducci for helpful criticisms and suggestions, and to Georgia Irby-Massie of Louisiana State University, whose proofreading and questioning greatly facilitated the final stages of this project.

ʄoɾɛwoɾd

○ ◑ ◐ ● ◐ ◑ ○

Book One and Apuleius' *Metamorphoses*

Most of Book One of Apuleius' *Metamorphoses* is a "tale within a tale" related by a character, whose name we eventually find out is Aristomenes, to the narrator of the novel, whose name we eventually find out is Lucius. This story is a semi-autonomous tale, like numerous others in the novel; and the prologue to the work, indeed, states that what we are reading is a collection of such stories designed to titillate us. If someone read the tale of Aristomenes without continuing to read the rest of the novel, however, s/he would have a very incomplete sense of the kind of story the *Metamorphoses* is. For in addition to a series of amusing stories strung together by the narrator, the *Metamorphoses* has a main narrative storyline about how Lucius is turned into an ass by a magic potion, about his adventures as an ass, and about his eventual change back to human form. The final book of the novel, moreover, contains a startling religious conclusion to the adventures of Lucius that forces us to rethink what we have come to believe about what we have been reading. Once we have read the whole novel, the narrative of Book One seems in retrospect to resonate broadly with what *now* seem to be major themes and ideas of the whole novel, although there is still considerable disagreement on what the novel is really all about.

Some critics, such as J. J. Winkler, argue that the novel's overall purpose has to do with this gap between expectation and fulfillment, between form and transformation, and that the tale of Aristomenes is a good example of the way Apuleius teases us readers in order to challenge us to rethink how and what we know. Indeed, with its odd mixture of terrifying witches and slapstick comedy, this tale is typical of much of the *Metamorphoses*. The tale is amusing, bizarre and surprising—not least because it ends up being not only a story *by* Aristomenes, but also a story *about* Aristomenes, who becomes an exile as a result of the events of the story he tells. In Winkler's terms, Aristomenes is both *auctor* and *actor*, both narrator and character. For someone familiar with the final book of the *Metamorphoses*, this outcome is not just surprising, but potentially significant; for the "I" of the whole novel (Lucius) not only narrates a whole series of amusing stories as he promises to do in the prologue—if indeed that is the same person—but is also the "me" of the novel; for he is also the narrator of his own transformation into an ass and his miraculous religious transformation at the end. Just as Aristomenes makes no mention at the beginning of the fact that this was also a story that led to his own transformation into an exile, so also Lucius makes no reference in the first ten books of the *Metamorphoses* to the fact that the outcome of his asinine adventures will be a religious conversion. The tale of Aristomenes can thus be seen as an anticipation of the shape of the entire *Metamorphoses* along with its serious conclusion.

But I have leapt "into the middle of things" by beginning my discussion of Book One with the tale of Aristomenes, for that semi-autonomous tale is situated in a narrative context that is just as surprising and problematic as the relationship of the tale to the whole novel. A critical discussion of Apuleius' text must consider a number of issues of literary production and tradition: the biography of Apuleius, the literary heritage of the *Metamorphoses*, the religious and philosophical context of Apuleius, and the narratological conventions that structure the novel, beginning with the prologue. But my "leap" into the middle of Book One is not so unusual for a discussion of Apuleius, for it is a text for which a whole swarm of issues and questions vie immediately and simultaneously for the attention of the reader. In fact it has been noted that the first words of the prologue (*At ego tibi...*) open as if in the middle of a conversation. Indeed, the overriding impression one gets of the flow of the *Metamorphoses* is a kind of headlong rush forwards that periodically and inconsistently glances backward to make tantalizing programmatic and interpretative statements that are elusive traces of meaning and purpose. Given this situation, interpretations of the novel must usually achieve consistency by ignoring certain things. Deciding what the novel is "really all about" thus often involves a certain "leap of faith;" but that might also be what the novel is all about. In this essay I will try to survey the kinds of approaches to the novel that have been most important, paying special attention to their pertinence to Book One.

As noted in the introduction above, most of what we know about Apuleius is derived from his own works. As is often the case with Apuleius, details of his life seem to have tantalizing connections with his novel, but it is often difficult to know what to make of them. Certainly his trial for casting a spell on his wife seems a possible reason for composing a story in which playing with magic has devastating consequences. His career as an orator giving speeches in Latin and Greek associates him with the "second sophistic," a contemporary literary movement which sought to revive the glories of traditional Greek culture, especially the glory of Greek rhetoric.[1] His peculiar literary style, full of archaisms and unusual words, is no doubt due to the influence of this literary movement. His compilations and learned discussions of philosophical topics show that he had a keen interest in Platonic philosophy. All of these facts may be significant for a critical assessment of the *Metamorphoses*, but it is difficult to say how significant. Is the *Metamorphoses* a philosophical narrative that promotes Platonic ideas? Is it a cautionary tale about magic based in some way on Apuleius' own bad experiences? Or is it a "sophistic" display of learning with no higher purpose than erudite entertainment?

---

[1] For Apuleius' relationship to the second sophistic see G. Sandy, *The Greek World of Apuleius* (Leiden, 1997), and Harrison 2000.

The prologue states that the *Metamorphoses* is a "Greekish story" (*fabula Grae-canica*), and indeed there is another version of the story preserved in Greek among the works of Lucian, a contemporary of Apuleius. This work, called *Lucius or the Ass*, is much shorter than the *Metamorphoses*, but contains some passages that are almost identical, so that some relationship must exist between them. It appears that another longer version of the story also existed in Greek and was entitled *Metamorphoses*, and that *Lucius or the Ass* is an epitome of this version.[2] This longer version still existed in the middle ages, but is now lost. The similarities between Apuleius' novel and *Lucius or the Ass* are most economically explained by the assumption that both used this lost earlier work as a source. It is tempting to triangulate between the lost Greek *Metamorphoses*, *Lucius or the Ass*, and Apuleius' *Metamorphoses* in order to speculate about what Apuleius added or subtracted from his original, but in the end nothing too specific can be deduced from this enterprise. None of the inserted tales, such as the tale of Aristomenes in Book One, are represented in *Lucius or the Ass*, but that doesn't mean they weren't in the Greek *Metamorphoses*. Similarly, the end of *Lucius or the Ass* is comical, but that does not prove that the Greek *Metamorphoses* did not have a seri-ous ending like the *Metamorphoses*. The most that can be said is that Apuleius wrote his novel the way he did because it suited him to do so, irrespective of the sources that he used or transformed. However, Apuleius takes the trouble to introduce the information that this is a Greek story made into Latin and states in addition that this change of language (*vocis immutatio*) corresponds to the literary effort he is under-taking. Even without knowing anything about the Greek source, we are compelled to wonder about the significance of this multilingual heritage.

It is traditional to call the *Metamorphoses* a novel, along with Petronius' *Satyri-con*, although the two works share little resemblance to each other, much less to the "Greek novels" which are roughly contemporary with them. Another generic term seems to be set forth in the first sentence of the prologue with the words *sermone Milesio*, which refer to certain erotic stories made famous by Aristides of Miletus, whose work is completely lost. The prologue promises to "string together" a series of such amusing stories for the delight of the reader. Later the term *Melesiae* is used again in reference to the lengthy inserted tale about Cupid and Psyche, related by an old woman (4.32). These references to Milesian tales strike most readers of the *Metamorphoses* as misleading: the novel turns to be much more than just a stringing together of erotic stories, and the tale of Cupid and Psyche, with its allegorical over-tones, seems to be much more than a Milesian tale. One lesson from this is that when the author makes explicit statements about what kind of story the *Metamorphoses* is we should not take them too seriously as articulations of a global strategy. But the question remains, What kind of story is this?

Extended prose fiction was never explicitly conceptualized as a literary genre in antiquity. Indeed, such works usually combine elements from numerous traditional genres in order to concoct a literary product that is more heterogeneous than any of its predecessors in antiquity. One inevitable consequence of this mixing of styles and genres is humor and parody. To juxtapose serious and comic elements, or humble

---

[2] For these Greek sources see H. Mason, "The *Metamorphoses* of Apuleius and its Greek Sources," in Hofmann 1999.

and lofty language, calls attention to the artificial and mannered character of literary conventions. The *Metamorphoses* of Apuleius is certainly such a hybrid mixture of literary types: comedy and tragedy, myth and folk-tale, epic and history, philosophy and satire. This multiplicity of forms contributes to the confusion about the novel, since these genres imply different and partly incompatible visions of meaning and reality. M. Bakhtin, who has written extensively on the modern novel and its ancient predecessors, argues that what separates the novel from other genres is the way it puts other literary styles and types into a "dialogue" with each other by juxtaposing them.

> "To a greater or lesser extent, every novel is a dialogized system made up of images of 'languages,' styles and consciousnesses that are concrete and inseparable from language. Language in the novel not only represents, but itself serves as the object of representation. Novelistic discourse is always criticizing itself."[3]

That the *Metamorphoses* is such a "dialogic" work is reflected in descriptive terms like "serio-comic" or "philosophical comedy." The story of the ass-man, derived from the Greek source, is the main narrative frame of the novel into which a bewildering variety of materials have been incorporated. Accounting for this multiplicity makes it nearly impossible to pigeon-hole the *Metamorphoses* with a convenient tag. At the same time, Apuleius' choice of "form"—using that word loosely—means that he can go about his business with as little restriction as possible on what he can or can't do.

In another essay Bakhtin studies different forms of time, which he uses to create a typology of various sorts of narrative.[4] One type he calls the "adventure novel of ordeal," in which an initial happy state (usually marriage) is interrupted by a series of adventures until the initial state is reestablished. This "adventure time" is abstract in the sense that the passing of time leaves no trace: the two lovers are the same before and after the series of adventures. The *Metamorphoses* is the model of another type, the "adventure novel of everyday life," which also has a potentially unlimited number of adventures, but is grounded in a developmental plot which leads from guilt to retribution, redemption, and blessedness. The individual episodes, however, and especially the inserted stories, display a kind of "everyday time;" seamy and obscene, fragmented and cut off from the rhythms of nature and the norms of society. This everyday time is not parallel to the developmental trajectory of the novel, but "intersects it at right angles" (Bakhtin, 128). The adventures of Lucius function to give concreteness to his experience by making it correspond to an actual course of travel. He travels, observing and revealing the private lives of others, experiencing life from the outside, and the sum of this experience constitutes a kind of "descent" into the underworld. Bakhtin thus acknowledges the disparity between the seriousness of Lucius' story of guilt and redemption, on the one hand, and the comic aspects of Lucius' misadventures, on the other, but subsumes the latter under the former, which is the basic position of all religious or moral interpretations of the novel.

---

[3] M. Bakhtin, *The Dialogic Imagination*, tr. C. Emerson and M. Holquist (Texas, 1981). p. 49.
[4] M. Bakhtin, "Forms of Time and Chronotope in the Novel," in *The Dialogic Imagination* (n. 3) 84–129.

Religious or moral interpretations of the novel have the last word, so to speak, because the story ends with a religious message. However, their main drawback is that the vast majority of the book seems strangely devoid of any religious or moral content. It is possible, upon closer look, to find traces of moral fiber in the first ten books of the novel, but this sometimes requires real ingenuity. For example, Tatum notes the tale of Aristomenes presents the themes of curiosity (*curiositas*), base pleasure (*voluptas*), and the fickleness of fortune (*fortuna*) in a way that is consistent with their presentation and relevance to Lucius in Book 11 (Tatum 1969). The harrowing tale of Aristomenes, with its lust, magic, and witches, is thought to be a warning to Lucius which he subsequently ignores, as he plunges into a hot sexual relationship in order to gain access to forbidden knowledge. The vice of *curiositas* gives a plausible basis for a moral interpretation of the story, especially since it seems to be an Apuleian coinage to translate the Platonic term *polypragmosyne*, "meddlesomeness."[5] But such moral interpretations do not seem adequately to account for the incongruity between the playfulness of tone with which all this seriousness is presented. Moral sentiment and judgment are certainly evoked in the novel frequently, but if that is what the novel is "really all about," it has been set forth in a very peculiar way.

Religious interpretations of the text usually focus on the figure of Isis, the Egyptian goddess who appears in a dream in Book 11 to lead Lucius into a new life. Isis is a goddess of "resurrection," who raised from the dead her brother and husband, Osiris, after he had been murdered by their enemy Set, whose association with the form of an ass makes that animal "most hateful" to Isis (*Met.* 11.6). Since the religion of Isis in imperial times was a "mystery" religion, with secrets and symbols, it has been argued that the peculiarities of the novel can only be properly understood when "decoded" by religious initiates.[6] So, for example, the ludicrous incident that ends Book One, where the fish Lucius buys for dinner is destroyed by an irate official as a punishment to the fishmonger for overcharging, has been linked with a ritual trampling of fish in certain Egyptian temples (Scobie 1975: 127). That the novel is some kind of systematic coding of religious content under a "veil" of allegorical indirection has won few adherents, but there is no doubt that contemporary religious and philosophical ideas are important cultural resources upon which Apuleius draws to give a serious resonance to his story. Thus the white horse (*peralbo equo*) Lucius rides in Book One, which reappears at the end with the name Candidus, has been seen as a Platonic symbol of philosophy.[7] The witch Meroe in the tale of Aristomenes, whose name perhaps recalls an important center of Isis worship, is the first of a series of powerful female figures that seem to culminate in some way in the epiphany of Isis in Book 11. However, if these serious meanings were paramount in Apuleius' mind, he made it difficult for us readers to grasp them on a casual reading of the novel.

Nancy Shumate takes another approach to the religious content by arguing that the novel tries to invoke the experience of conversion, an experience that is prompted

---

[5] DeFilippo 1990; J. Penwill, "Slavish Pleasures and Profitless Curiosity: Fall and Redemption in Apuleius' *Metamorphoses*," *Ramus* 4 (1975), 49–82.

[6] G. Griffiths, *The Isis Book of the Metamorphoses.* Leiden, 1975.

[7] G. Drake, "Candidus, A Unifying Theme in Apuleius' Metamorphoses," *Classical Journal* 64 (1968), 102–09.

by a series of existential crises.[8] Lucius' transformation into an ass forces him to see himself and his world from a new angle and this reevaluation concludes when he turns forever from his old life and is "born again" into a new life. Such an invocation of the conversion experience does not mean that the text is an authentic autobiography in the mode of St. Augustine's *Confessions* (indeed, it is a far cry from such works), but presents this religious experience while simultaneously critiquing it, without ever decisively taking one side or the other. Shumate argues that the reader is left to make his or her own decision about the validity of religious experience. This reading partially coincides with Winkler's view of the novel as a "philosophical comedy about religious knowledge" since both focus on the indeterminacies in the text caused by the hermeneutic playfulness of the author and his narrators. Apuleius seems to be peculiarly resistant to providing definitive versions of moral judgment and interpretation, and this resistance seems to dovetail with a number of narratological peculiarities in the story, to which we must now turn.

The key issue can be summarized by two words from the prologue: *quis ille*? "Who is that?"[9] The prologue begins with someone encouraging us readers to enjoy the tales he is about to tell us. This narrator claims to be of Greek origin and to have learned Latin with some difficulty, so this is a fictive narrator not to be identified with the North African Apuleius. After the prologue, the story begins, again with a first person narrator whom we eventually discover is named Lucius and is from Corinth. It is never made crystal clear whether this Lucius, who turns out to be telling <u>his</u> story, is different from or the same as the speaker in the prologue, the one who had promised to "string together" tales of transformation in a *sermone Milesio*; but a scrupulous comparison suggests that they are not the same.[10] In the final book of the novel, moreover, a priest of Osiris is told in a dream to seek out and purify the protagonist, who is identified in this dream as Lucius of Madaura, which tradition identifies as Apuleius' hometown, but in any case is the hometown of neither Lucius nor the prologue speaker. There is really no way to eliminate completely these inconsistencies, although there have been many interesting attempts to explain these and many other apparent lapses of consistency in narrative voice.[11] It is possible, of course, that Apuleius just goofed, but there is a great deal else in the novel that makes it seem that he intended these riddles to provoke and tease the reader. To what purpose?

Winkler argues that the *Metamorphoses* is a kind of intellectual training ground where a scrupulous reader will come to recognize that no knowledge, not even the religious knowledge espoused at the end, is firmly authorized. By attaching primary importance to these narratological issues, he sees in Apuleius' very inconsistency another kind of consistency more important than Isis, philosophy, or morality. Although Winkler has clearly shown us something important about the *Metamorphoses*, his interpretation of the novel requires a certain leap of faith, since there is

---

[8] Nancy Shumate, *Crisis and Conversion* (Ann Arbor, 1996).
[9] Winkler 1985 is the key discussion for these narratological issues.
[10] See Harrison 1990; Laird 1993.
[11] R. T. van der Paardt, "The Unmasked 'I': *Met.* 11.27," *Mnemosyne* 34 (1981), 96–106; and Smith 1972, both reprinted in Harrison 1999; Dowden 1982; and Edwards 1993.

something circular and paradoxical about speaking of "convention-breaking shifts as regular, as the predictable or characteristic behavior" of the *Metamorphoses* (Winkler 175). No more (or less) certain is Harrison's position that the entire novel, including Book 11, is the kind of erudite entertainment typical of sophistic display, with no serious message at all (Harrison 2000). What makes the *Metamorphoses* so maddening and so seductive is that we are given so little help in deciding how scrupulously we should read this text, in deciding whether something odd is a careless inconsistency or whether Apuleius, like Pee Wee Herman, "meant to do that."

Stephen Harrison has argued that the identity of the prologue is not a person at all, but the physical book itself, an example of the "talking book" theme of which there are other examples in Latin literature (Harrison 1990). Although this approach is not entirely satisfying either, it does make an important point about the *Metamorphoses* and novels in general. When we read an "ego" in a written text we immediately begin to speculate about the identity of this "I" and assume that it must represent some person or thing, just as the "tibi" must represent us readers. This is based on the analogy of live interaction or live performances, in which all that is spoken emanates from a represented "person" that temporarily inhabits a particular body. But in a text that is not organized around a performer—and this is the smaller part of what we call ancient literature—the "I" and "you" can be just textual markers that establish temporary relationships within the world of the text without necessarily being grounded in anything "outside" it. The stability of a *performing presence* is replaced by another sort of stability centered around the *reader's activity*. As we continue to read, speculating and modifying our sense of who is who, our activity as readers confers a certain concreteness on these textual identities. If we are looking, they must be there to be found! It is important to recognize, however, that there need not really "be" a person or thing that is the source of the "ego" in the first sentence of the prologue, or even the "ego" in the first sentence after the prologue. The indirectness of the answer the prologue gives to the question "quis ille?" initiates a deferral of specificity that never really ends in the novel. At the same time, Apuleius provides just enough consistency to create a minimum of plausibility, and holds out just enough promise of eventual illumination to keep the reader continuing to look for definitive answers. Whatever effects the novel achieves depends on the reader accepting this impossible mission.[12]

There is another point about the prologue of the *Metamorphoses* that has special relevance to the first book of the novel: when was the prologue written? It is certainly a reasonable assumption that prologues and introductions are written last, when it is possible to know exactly what it is one must introduce, and this is the attested practice of a number of authors from antiquity.[13] However, isn't it possible that the prologue was written first or at least near the beginning, at a point when the author had only a general idea what he was going to write about, with the bulk of the novel only vaguely outlined, along with a multiplicity of possible purposes and outcomes? This question has special relevance to Book One because there is slim lexical evidence

---

[12] For a minimum of "plausibility" as the narrator's goal, see Dowden 1982. For Apuleius' inducements to the reader to continue seeking answers, see Winkler 60–9.

[13] T. Janson, *Latin Prose Prefaces* (Stockholm, 1964), 73–74.

that Book One may have been composed a good deal earlier than the rest of the novel (Scobie 1975: 24–25). Even if that is not so, *something* had to be composed first and what was composed later may not have been written in entirely the same spirit. The more general question raised here is to what degree we should assume that the same purpose(s) are infused homogeneously throughout the entire work. When discussing a particular passage, literary critics typically take for granted that the rest of the novel is always already written, and hence that it is possible to read backwards and forwards from any point to find correlation for a particular interpretation. A more realistic assumption might be that the process of composing the work itself modified the author's purposes, or added to them. Book One of the *Metamorphoses* is a good example of the way surprising things seem to emerge from the events of the story according to rules that are being formulated and modified as we go along. Ellen Finkelpearl suggests that the key trajectory of the novel is not the transformation and redemption of Lucius, but the evolution and metamorphosis of the novel itself as a genre (Finkelpearl 1998). Her thesis is attractive in that it seeks not to explain inconsistency in the work by finding some more recondite consistency, but sees the novel as a *project,* something that is becoming what it is in the very process of its composition.

A related point is made by Judith Krabbe, who observes that the relationship among various thematic elements in the novel are best described as *immutatio,* the closest Latin word to the Greek word *metamorphosis,* and the very word used in the prologue to describe the novel's "change of language" from Greek to Latin (*vocis immutatio*).[14] But *immutatio,* she notes, is also the Latin translation from Greek of the rhetorical term metonymy (literally "change of name"), a basic form of figurative language by which things associated with something become substituted for them, such as *Venerem habere* = "to have sex." Metonymy relies on existing networks of connections among words (Venus is the goddess of sexual pleasure), but innovative figures of speech can also create new networks by positing new connections. Apuleius' *Metamorphoses* seems to be a world where new and unusual connections are being fabricated, not just where already established ones are being rehearsed. The linear unfolding of the narrative is like a series of "mutations," variations of scenes and themes growing out of each other, "things becoming other by association or contiguity" (Kraabe, 144). The last word of the *Metamorphoses, obibam,* is an imperfect indicative: "I was going about...." Just as the opening, "At ego tibi...," seems to start in the middle of a conversation, the end is not a traditional closure, which would require a perfect tense ("and that's how I came to be who I am today"), but seems to imply that more *immutationes* are to come.[15]

The literary fortunes of the *Metamorphoses* itself have undergone *immutationes* as remarkable as its hero Lucius. Once reviled as a patchwork resulting from Apuleius' "desultory psychosis" (Perry 1967), the novel has more recently been hailed as a masterpiece of intricate structure and ingenuity. If Perry's unsympathetic view of Apuleius is based inappropriately on expectations of narrative "unity" derived from the criticism of modern fiction, the view of Apuleius as the James Joyce of antiquity

---

[14] J. Krabbe, *The Metamorphoses of Apuleius* (New York, 1989), p. 144.
[15] For the "imperfect" ending, see Winkler, 223–27.

is equally problematic. A more moderate position is represented by Carl Schlam, who sees the action of the plot to be neither "tightly organized nor entirely chaotic," with a kind of coherence resulting from an "abundant network of themes" connecting the stories so that they make "continuous commentary on themselves and on each other" (Schlam 1992: 6). In such a text it is a dubious strategy to take small selections of the story as a "part for the whole." Book One is an appropriate introduction to the *Metamorphoses* only so long as we consider it in all its exuberant heterogeneity.

It is true, for example, that Book One sets out several key thematic elements that can be followed throughout the story: the danger of *curiositas*, the changeability of fortune, and the connection between magic and sensual pleasure. But the presentation of these themes in the tale of Aristomenes—with its mixture of serious and comic and its toying with appearance and reality—keeps us in suspense about the future of these ideas in the novel. Moreover, that tale itself is situated in an inconclusive discussion of the veracity of tales of magic, in which a contrast is drawn between the skepticism of Aristomenes' unnamed companion and the indiscriminate credulity of Lucius. We are invited to believe that things are more than they seem, but also to jeer at the gullibility of Lucius, who believes that all things are possible. Such internal commentary on aspects of story-telling occurs throughout the *Metamorphoses*, which makes it seem we are overhearing Apuleius thinking out loud about what he is doing. Before Aristomenes tells his story, his companion produces a hackneyed list of the exploits of witches, sneering at such nonsense. However, in the tale itself a similar list of exploits is attributed to Meroe by her erstwhile victim, and vouched for by the experience of Aristomenes himself. This casual seepage between the main narrative frame and the stories within that frame occurs again and again in the *Metamorphoses*, blurring the boundaries between the *lepidas fabulas* and the account of Lucius' transformation, making us wonder what is frame and what is being framed.

The final episode of Book One, the trampling of the fish by the market official, is the kind of peculiar incident that cries out for some explanation for its inclusion in the story; but it is also like numerous other episodes that seem to go nowhere, whose inclusion seems to be a path followed for a while and then abandoned. By the time we realize this episode has gone nowhere, we have long replaced our question about its meaning with numerous others that seem more pressing and pertinent. Is it possible to read the banal ending of this episode as a reflection of some characteristic of the entire novel, just as we read the surprise ending of the tale of Aristomenes to be an anticipation of the novel's surprise ending?

The narrator mentions early on his relationship by blood to the Greek author Plutarch, an important contemporary literary figure who wrote a philosophical commentary on the religion of Isis and Osiris. Is this a clue about the philosophical character of the story? an anticipation of its Isiac conclusion? or a hint about its literary heritage in the revival of Greek learning in which Plutarch played a role? Although it could be one or all of these things, it is equally pertinent that we still do not even know the narrator's name at this point; much less that the story is about to "morph" into an autobiography that will be much more than what the prologue promised. Apuleius' stinginess about crucial information, so well detailed by Winkler and others, is regularly accompanied by a surplus of *potentially* significant clues and insinuation, thematic correspondences that are "too exact to be accidental, too extraneous to be significant" (Winkler 118). One effect of this baffling combination is that Apuleius has a maximum amount of flexibility as the story unfolds to revise his purposes while maintaining continuity with what preceded, to confer *retrospectively* meaning on what he has written by further elaboration. Book One is an appropriate beginning for many possible novels, only one of which Apuleius actually wrote. That readers are so uncertain what the novel is "all about" may be due to the fact that Apuleius' own answer to that question evolves and changes as the novel unfolds.

STEPHEN NIMIS
Miami University, Ohio
nimissa@muohio.edu

Introduction

The Author of the *Metamorphoses*

About the life of Apuleius, the author of our text, much can be said but little is certain. Many older books call him Lucius Apuleius, but this is a guess based on the name he assigns to his main character in the *Metamorphoses*, Lucius, who is transformed into an ass. While the author claims, near the end of the work, that the book is about himself, and even though the book is written in the first person and much of the content of the book comes from material that is clearly familiar to the author, in recent times it has been recognized that it is risky to assign specific pieces of that fictional tale to the actual life of the author himself. We are in fact much better informed about what he wrote and where he lived for a large part of his life, and indeed about what contemporary and subsequent readers thought of him, than what he did.

Even the name of his birthplace, Madauros (in north Africa), is based on that reference by the fictional Lucius in Book 11 (ch. 27: *et de eius ore, quo singulorum facta dictat, audisse mitti sibi Madaurensem, sed admodum pauperem, cui statim sua sacra deberet ministrare*, "[the priest] had heard from the mouth of the [statue], by which it declares the deeds of individuals, that a man from Madauros was being sent to him, though he was very poor, to whom he must provide his rites"); this information, though somewhat problematic (Lucius is described as very poor, while Apuleius elsewhere claims to have been well off), is generally regarded as true, since many later writers refer to him as *Platonicus Madaurensis philosophus*, "the Platonist philosopher from Madauros."

A great many of the details about his personal life are extracted from the published version of a speech that he gave in his own defense, the *Apologia*, when he had been indicted for practicing magic to bewitch a wealthy widow, Aemilia Pudentilla, whom he had married in Africa in 157 at the urging of her son, one Pontianus, who had studied with Apuleius in Athens. According to Apuleius, the marriage was arranged to protect Pudentilla's fortune, but other members of the family interpreted events differently and indicted him on various charges, including witchcraft, in 158 or 159 before the proconsul of Africa. It is perhaps overly skeptical to doubt the reality of this trial, though the *Apologia* betrays no sense of anxiety about his fate, and the speech is filled with digression that illustrates his wit and learning rather than evidence of his innocence.

On the basis of the dates for these events, which are secure within a narrow range, it has been deduced that Apuleius was born about 125. Apuleius had inherited a substantial fortune, studied in Carthage and Athens, and taught rhetoric in Rome for an unknown period of time, before returning to Africa. He lists Samos and Phrygia among his travels, in addition to Athens, Rome, Carthage, and Alexandria. Passages from his later speeches, collected as the *Florida*, show that he spent some years in Carthage in the 160s, where he had a distinguished reputation, as evidenced by a statue erected in his honor and a position as a priest in the imperial cult. His description of Lucius's epiphany in Book 11 of the *Metamorphoses*, as well as his travel to Alexandria and interest in things Egyptian, support the claim that he was also an advanced initiate in the cult of Isis. Among the works ascribed to him are two, *De Mundo* ("On the World") and *De Platone* ("On Plato"), which are addressed to a son named Faustinus, but the authorship of these books is disputed. There are no certain references to Apuleius after the 160s, so that it is not known how he spent his later years or when he died.

Apuleius apparently called the story of Lucius the *Metamorphoses* ("Transformations"), though later writers referred to it as the *Golden Ass*. The basic plot was simple, and apparently borrowed from a Greek work entitled *Lucius, or the Ass*. Apuleius added in a large number of stories and fables, some more directly relevant to the main tale than others. In our story Lucius is a businessman, or merchant, on his way to Thessaly for professional reasons. Because of his uncontrollable curiosity, especially about magic, he is transformed into an ass. He retains his human understanding, but is unable to use human speech. He tries to find roses, which will allow him to be changed back into human form if he eats them. In his adventures, he is mistreated in various ways by various humans, and numerous stories arise about Lucius or about other characters in the work; the most famous of these tales is the story of Cupid and Psyche, which begins in Book 4 and continues well into Book 6. These stories form the bulk of Apuleius' additions to the basic story line, on which there has been considerable study. Apuleius also added an unexpected chapter in a final Book, in which Lucius experiences an epiphany of the goddess Isis, and through her intervention is changed back into human form, after which he becomes an initiate into her cult.

In Book 1, we are introduced to Lucius, though his name is not revealed till very late in the Book. One story is recounted in Book 1, the Tale of Aristomenes, which is told not by Lucius, but by a stranger he has met by chance; there is a third (unnamed) character, evidently a friend of Aristomenes, who plays the role of skeptic to Lucius' credulity in regards to this tale. There is little in Book 1 that leads us to believe that the work as a whole will contain a religious message. The issue of the credibility of miraculous events is raised, but not seriously answered in this Book: the argument is not concluded, since the three characters reach their destination and go their separate ways. But by engaging this story, and the reactions of Lucius and the skeptic, the reader is prepared gradually for the increasingly marvelous stories of the later Books. For a theoretical treatment of the narrative of Book 1, I am grateful to Stephen Nimis of Miami University (Ohio) for writing the Foreword.

Apuleius' Latin

Apuleius' style defies any single categorization. Words like "ebullient" and "idiosyncratic" figure prominently in any attempt to describe it. You will find that his vocabulary is often eccentric: he often uses ordinary words in senses that are unusual (such as *commodum* in the sense of *modo*), or in senses that are new to him (such as *denique* to mean, "for example"); he sprinkles his text liberally with so-called archaisms, that is, words that have fallen out of fashion or general use (such as *exanclare*, "endure," or *sublimare*, "raise up"); he frequently uses words that do not appear at all before him (such as *scissillus*, "tattered," and *palliastrum*, "cloak"); and he uses a wide variety of compounds of the same verb, evidently simply for variety (such as of -*ducere* and -*cedere*). Often, he presses the meanings of words to their limits. Most of these oddities are noted in the commentary; in addition, words in the reading are glossed rather generously, in order to save time looking them up, but in any case the general glossary at the end contains all the words that occur in Book One. Apuleius' syntax is periodic, but balanced: his sentences average about 20 words each, but the parts are often coordinated and parallel, rather than subordinated or involuted. (In technical language, Apuleius' syntax is "paratactic" rather than "hypotactic.") Given the content of his book, it is not surprising that he would want the general style to have a conversational flavor, and he does indeed use many colloquialisms, words from daily life, diminutive forms (which often add emotional color), and redundant expressions. But his style is by no means colloquial: he also uses solemn words and expressions, and occasional forays into high rhetorical style. In fact, his style, while sounding natural and effusive, is quite artificial, and heavily stylized; it is, indeed, his own creation, a special idiom all his own for which the rules—such as they are— emerge as we read. (For the connections between Apuleius' style and "Asianism," see Purser lxxxiv–xcvi, and Kenney 1990, 28–38).

Notes for the Instructor

This edition is intended for undergraduates in approximately the fourth university semester. Apuleius' Latin is eccentric, but not grammatically difficult, and the content is entertaining. As a first unadapted author, or as part of a combination of unadapted texts, the first book of Apuleius' *Metamorphoses* makes a fine choice. The notes are therefore entirely geared to the intermediate undergraduate, not to the scholar. They are intended to facilitate relatively fast reading and to call attention to grammatical points that are ordinarily given special treatment in the second year.

On matters of interpretation, I have tried mainly to provide sign-posts for fruitful thought by students, not to impose a specific reading of the text. In this regard, I confess, I have found Winkler and Schlam particularly helpful, regardless of whether one subscribes to their final interpretation of the author. On the whole, this approach requires us to be attentive and informed first readers, such that we can appreciate the direction of the story at the moment, and recall it for later re-interpretation as subsequent information is provided. Except for the conviction that in reading a book it is good to start at the beginning, I am pursuing no interpretive agenda. At the same time, I have tried to show students that meaning may have to be found below the surface, and I have tried not to make the commentary useless for those who do wish to treat interpretive issues with their students at this level.

I have avoided, except for comments in the general introduction (above), the issue of Apuleius' source or model, because I find that it distracts students at this level from the flow of the story; instructors who prefer to treat this question can and will certainly do so in their own way. (Similarly, I have in general avoided using Greek, since Latin students at this level cannot be presumed to know it; where Greek is used for illustrative or explanatory purposes, it is always both transliterated and translated, if necessary.)

Apuleius has benefitted (and continues to benefit) in this century from the attention of outstanding critics, and the works cited in the bibliography will repay attention. References to scholarship, except for editors of the text, are confined to works in English. The selected readings at the end of the book, all in English and all readily available, should provide a useable basis for further reading or for assignments from the instructor. On the other hand, scholarly attention has—relatively speaking—been disproportionately meager on Book 1. While the tide has shifted a bit in recent years, scholars who treat the *Metamorphoses* have largely been interested in the Cupid and Psyche story or in the meaning of Book 11; where attention has been devoted to Book 1, a high percentage of it has been on the Prologue.

We are doubly fortunate, therefore, to have two full scholarly commentaries on Book 1, a 1938 Groningen dissertation by Margaretha Molt (in Latin), and A. Scobie's 1975 commentary, written in English. While neither is easily accessible to, or intended for use by, undergraduates, I have obviously made heavy use of both. Moreover, the popular English editions of the Cupid and Psyche story by Purser and Kenney both have much that is useful for a general appreciation of Apuleius's language and style, and scholars will also note reflections of their work in the notes.

The text printed here is closely based upon R. Helm's second Teubner edition, used here with the permission of K.G. Saur Verlag, which now owns the rights to Teubner publications; the edition used was R. Helm, *Apulei Metamorphoseon Libri XI, Lipsiae in Aedibus Teubneri*, 1913, pp. 1–24. I have made a few changes in punctuation and orthography, and have reformatted paragraphs, all with a view toward clarity for reading. At difficult points in the text where Helm had brackets indicating deletion or insertion, I have usually deleted or inserted without retaining brackets, or any other special visual aids to indicate difficulty with the text. Nor have I included an *apparatus criticus*, which would have delayed this project considerably. I have, however, tried to give very full attention in the notes to the most important places where editors have struggled with the text. I have especially tried to explain to students not only what the text that they are reading says, but what the problems are (or might be) and what the implications of proposed solutions are, none of which is in fact easy for students to glean from an *apparatus*. In this process I have referred to numerous text editors, but I list only Helm and Hanson in the bibliography, since Helm's text is before us and Hanson wrote in English; the lack of bibliographical reference to other editors might require an early comment from the instructor.

Apuleius

○ ○ ◐ ● ◑ ○ ○

The Metamorphoses
Book 1

Apuleius
The Metamorphoses, Book One

The book may be divided for convenience into five parts, some of which may be further subdivided as shown:

A. Prologue (1)

B. Lucius meets two fellow-travelers (2–4)

C. The tale of Aristomenes (5–19)
1. Aristomenes meets Socrates and hears of his misfortunes (5–7)
2. Socrates explains that he has been cursed by a witch (8–10)
3. The witches attack Socrates (11–13)
4. Aristomenes tries to escape (14–16)
5. Socrates revives, and the two friends leave the inn (17)
6. The curse of the witches is fulfilled (18–19)

D. Arrival in Hypata (20–21)

E. At the house of Milo (22–26)
1. Arrival and introductions (22–23)
2. Side-trip to the market (24–25)
3. A long evening with Milo (26)

Apulei Madaurensis
Metamorphoseon, Liber I

[1]   At ego tibi sermone isto Milesio varias fabulas conseram,

2   auresque tuas benivolas lepido susurro permulceam — modo

[1]

The Prologue (1). As often in a Latin work, the first sentence or paragraph contains a kind of introduction to the whole work. In the first section of Apuleius' book, he provides clues as to his method and narrative style (*sermone...Milesio*), and, as we discover, to the identity of the narrator. But his information about the narrator, although told in the first person, remains indistinct for some time, and it is only at the end of the book (1.24 [line 499]) that we finally find out that his name is Lucius.

1. at: the book begins as if in the middle of a conversation; the narrator is objecting to or picking up on a point made by someone else. Scobie notes that, while *at* is infrequently used by others to begin sentences (indeed, Apuleius does this several times in Book 1), its use to begin an entire book is unique.

sermone isto Milesio: "in your Milesian mode of conversing," i.e., in the manner of a "Milesian tale," with entertaining and erotic episodes loosely stitched together. (This novelistic form was called "Milesian" from the title Μιλησιακά [*Milesiaka*] by the Greek Aristides in the second century BCE, and the *Milesian Tales* of L. Cornelius Sisenna

in the first century BCE.) Apuleius has a particular fondness for *iste*, which often differs little from a plain demonstrative (like *ille*).

conseram: "I would (like to) stitch together," the conclusion (apodosis), along with *permulceam*, of a conditional clause; the protasis is *si...non spreveris*. The stitched-together-ness (a metaphor from weaving) of the *Metamorphoses* is one of its charms as well as a challenge to the critic who tries to understand it; the best continuous presentation of this feature of the work is Schlam 1992.

2. lepido susurro: "with an elegant murmur." *lepidus* (as a description of literary style) indicates that the work will be carefully written, pleasurable to read (or hear), and erudite, "charming;" *susurrus* here simply means soft tones, but later (1.3. [line 41]) the word *susurramen* is used of a magical incantation, so that this connotation is also present.

permulceam: the basic claim for the stories told in the book is that they bring pleasure and relaxation. Tatum 1969 has confirmed what many believe, however, that most of the tales in the book are also cautionary and ultimately edifying.

si papyrum Aegyptiam argutia Nilotici calami inscriptam non spreveris inspicere —, figuras fortunasque hominum in alias

5   imagines conversas et in se rursum mutuo nexu refectas ut mireris.

Exordior. Quis ille? Paucis accipe. Hymettos Attica et Isthmos Ephyrea et Taenaros Spartiaca, glebae felices aeternum libris felicioribus conditae, mea vetus prosapia est.

---

3. papyrum Aegyptiam: while this may be a reference to the author's residence in Alexandria, it can also be read as either redundant or as a reference to source and quality (Scobie 69).

argutia Nilotici calami: "the sharpness of the Nilish pen" (instead of "the sharp Nilish pen"). The choice of *argutia* reinforces the claim of the work to stylistic sharpness and subtelty.

4. spreveris: 2d, s., perfect subjunctive of *spernĕre.*

figuras fortunasque hominum in alias imagines conversas: in effect, a rendering or explanation of the title of the book, *Metamorphoses*; this rendering explains that not all of the transformations will be physical, but that change in fortune will also be a topic for stories.

figuras...ut mireris: a purpose clause.

7. exordior: the narrator now tells us some things about himself, but by no means a great deal; more details emerge as the story proceeds.

quis ille?: "Who (is) that (speaking, you ask)?" Winkler 1985 argues that this question, the identity of the narrator, is pervasive and fundamental to an understanding of the work as a whole. That Apuleius withholds Lucius' name until nearly the end of Book 1 may also suggest that we are to suspend judgment on this question. Various critics have argued that the narrator of the Prologue is (or is not) Lucius (i.e., is the same as the main character), and is (or is not) to be thought of as Apuleius himself.

Hymettos...Isthmos...Taenaros: all nominative, singular, feminine (Greek second declension). Hymettus is the name of the mountain peak to the east of Athens, the Isthmus of Corinth is to the west, and Taenarus is a mountain in the southern Peloponnesus, near Sparta.

8. glebae felices: "fertile/fruitful clods," metonymy for *agri felices.* The use of *felix* in this agricultural sense is common, but Apuleius plays on the word almost immediately, *libris felicioribus,* "more cheerful/fruitful books." Even *liber* may be consistent in the agricultural word-play, since its original meaning was "(tree) bark." The use of the same word in different forms close together like this is called polyptoton; Apuleius is fond of this device.

9. prosapia: "stock, lineage," an archaic word. Apuleius is fond of archaisms.

10   Ibi linguam Attidem primis pueritiae stipendiis merui.
Mox in urbe Latia advena studiorum Quiritium indigenam
sermonem aerumnabili labore, nullo magistro praeeunte,
aggressus excolui. En ecce praefamur veniam, siquid exotici
ac forensis sermonis rudis locutor offendero. Iam haec
15   equidem ipsa vocis immutatio desultoriae scientiae stilo quem

10. primis...stipdendiis merui: all military language, "I served (in the Attic tongue) in my first (boyhood) tour of duty," i.e., I learned Greek as my first language.

11. advena: nominative, s., m., "as a stranger." This is the subject of *aggressus excolui*, "I approached and worked hard at." It is possible that *aggressus* continues the military language of the previous sentence, but *excolui* sets a different tone. The direct object is *indigenam sermonem*, "the native speech." *indigena* is an adjective that is always first declension, even when modifying a masculine (as here) or neuter noun. *studiorum Quiritium*: "of Roman studies." The narrator makes clear that he is not a native Roman, and that Latin is not his native language, but he had considerable Roman background.

12. praeeunte = *prae-eunte*: present participle < *prae-eo, prae-ire* (irreg.)

13. praefamur: "I beg in advance (for)." *veniam* < *venia, -ae* (f), "pardon." With *si...offendero, praefamur* forms an interesting mixed real condition: "I am now asking for forgiveness, if I shall (in the future) have offended." No significance should be attached to the variation between plural (*praefamur*) and singular (*offendero*).

exotici ac forensis sermonis: "strange (to me) speech of the (Roman) forum."

15. vocis immutatio: "change of language (into Latin)." But the phrase may have deeper resonance, "change of (narrator's) voice:" the narrator and the author need not be the same person, or *persona*.

stilo: ablative of means or cause, "by the pen (language)," i.e., he changes languages when he changes pens. The *stilus* proper was used to write in wax; perhaps we are meant to envision a letter rather than a literary work.

accessimus respondet. Fabulam Graecanicam incipimus.
Lector, intende: laetaberis.

[2]   Thessaliam — nam et illic originis maternae nostrae
fundamenta a Plutarcho illo inclito ac mox Sexto philosopho
20   nepote eius prodita gloriam nobis faciunt — eam Thessaliam

16. respondet = *correspondet*: "is like, resembles" + dative (*desultoriae scientiae*: a difficult phrase. *desultores* were riders in the Circus, who rode two horses together, leaping quickly from one to the other [see Liv. 23.9.5]; Apuleius means that his art consists in rapid changes of topic, and perhaps in style, without losing control, so that *desultoriae scientiae* should be rendered, "expertise in leaping back and forth." On this see Scobie 75f).

Graecanicam: Varro (*LL* 9.3) states that this means not "Greek" as such, but material that has been taken from

Greek and rendered into Latin. Hence, the word is used precisely here for the main tale that Apuleius has borrowed from a Greek original, modified, and enclosed or mixed within other tales of Latin type.

17. lector, intende: laetaberis: while this sort of admonition to the audience is common enough in Roman comedy, most critics argue that Apuleius has a more serious literary purpose: the Reader must pay close attention to get the most out of the book, and pleasure (or joy) will be the reward.

[2]

Strangers Meet on the Road (2–4). The narrator meets two strangers, who are in a discussion about reality and illusion. One stranger is a skeptic, and requires the evidence of his own eyes to believe in strange events, but the other is open-minded, and invites the narrator to express his own opinion.

18. nam...faciunt: the basic structure is *fundamenta (...prodita) gloriam nobis faciunt*.

originis maternae nostrae fundamenta: "the origin of my family on my mother's side."

19. (fundamenta) a Plutarcho illo incluto...prodita: "(the origin) which descends from the famous Plutarch." The narrator is given a distinguished family tree; we later learn (2.2) that his mother's name is Salvia, which connects her to a clan prominent in Thessaly during the Imperial Period. The connection to Plutarch, the famous author of the *Parallel Lives*, may refer to the influence on Apuleius himself of his neo-Platonic essays (Schlam 1992, 15–16). Sextus Plutarch(us) was Plutarch's nephew, a professional philosopher and mentor of Marcus Aurelius, as

ex negotio petebam. Postquam ardua montium et lubrica
vallium et roscida caespitum et glebosa camporum
emersimus, equo indigena peralbo vehens, iam eo quoque
admodum fesso, ut ipse etiam fatigationem sedentariam
25   incessus vegetatione discuterem, in pedes desilio, equi
sudorem frontem curiose effrico, aures remulceo, frenos

---

well as teacher of L. Aurelius Verus, who became emperor in 161.

21. ardua montium...lubrica vallium...roscida caespitum...glebosa camporum: all neuter plurals followed by defining genitives, "the rough (parts of the) mountains...the slippery (parts of the) valleys...the dewy (parts of the) meadows...the cloddy (parts of the) plains." Apuleius is fond of this kind of periphrasis; he could equally have written *arduos montes, lubricas valles*, etc.

23. iam eo...fesso: not an ablative absolute, since *equo*, to which *eo* refers, is already in the ablative where it appears earlier in the sentence. The usage *equo...vehens* ("riding on a horse") is a little unusual, but both Scobie and Molt cite Cicero (*Brutus* 97) and Gellius (5.26.7) for the intransitive sense of *veho* and for the absence of a preposition.

24. ut ipse...discuterem: a purpose clause.

25. incessus vegetatione: "by the invigoration of a walk." *incessūs* is genitive (4th declension).

26. sudorem frontem...effrico: this version of the text, which is found in the MSS and retained by Helm in his 2nd Teubner edition and by Hanson in his Loeb edition, requires a double accusative with *effrico* ("scrape the sweat [from] the

forehead"), a construction not found elsewhere with this verb. (Double accusatives are found with various Latin verbs, such as *flagitare aliquid aliquem*, "demand something [from] someone.") To avoid this, Haupt neatly suggested emending *sudorem* to *sudoram* ("sweaty"), an adjective that Apuleius used elsewhere (*Florida* 16). Helm (in his 3rd edition) changes *frontem* to *fronte*; this could be understood as an ablative of separation, "from the forehead": *frontem* was written *frontē* in the MSS, the stroke over the vowel being the ordinary abbreviation for the accusative, which could have been a simple scribal error. Molt cites Petronius 8.1 in support: *sudorem ille manibus detersit*. While various other emendations have been proposed, the only other that remains close to the original MSS is the emendation suggested by Becichem of *fronte* to *fronde*, "with a leaf."

aures remulceo: "I stroke his ears," explained by Molt (p. 4) as a means of removing the bridle (*frenos detraho* in the next clause), which was attached to the ears. She also, however, notes the similarity of the phrase to *aures permulceo*, one of the functions of storytelling given in the first sentence of the book by the narrator, and wonders (citing *remulcere* in this sense from 5.15) whether Apuleius suggests that the narrator "speaks comfortingly" to the horse.

detraho, in gradum lenem sensim proveho, quoad lassitudinis incommodum alvi solitum ac naturale praesidium eliquaret.

Ac dum is ientaculum ambulatorium, prata quae praeterit, ore in latus detorto, pronus affectat, duobus comitum, qui forte paululum processerant, tertium me facio. Ac dum ausculto quid sermonis agitarent, alter exserto cachinno "Parce, "inquit, "in verba ista haec tam absurda tamque immania mentiendo."

30

---

28. incommodum: accusative, s., n., "discomfort," is the direct object of *eliquaret*; the subjunctive is explained as a purpose construction after *quoad* ("until...might remove").

alvi solitum ac naturale praesidium: *praesidum* (nominative, s., n.) is the subject of *eliquaret*. *alvi...praesidium*, "the guard of his belly," as is made clear from the next sentence, is a periphrasis for *cibus*, "food," not (as early translators thought) for defecation.

29. prata quae praeterit: in apposition to *ientaculum ambulatorium* (direct object of *affectat*), "his walking meal, the meadows he passed by." The phrase adds specificity to the colorful *ientaculum ambulatorium*, and also plays on the sound *prata...praeterit*.

30. ore in latus detorto: ablative absolute, "with his mouth (face, head) twisted to his side" (*detorto < de+torquere*).

duobus comitum: ("to two *of* the fellow-travelers") instead of *duobus comitibus*.

32. quid sermonis: "what conversation." This genitive of the whole is the usual construction with indefinite quantities, and is often used in analogous situations, such as *quid novi*, "What's new?" Plautus, *Poenulus* 822 has an almost exact parallel, *quid habeat sermonis, auscultabo.*

exserto cachinno: "with a burst of laughter." In Apuleius, laughter is nearly always cruel or derisive; see Schlam 1992, 40–44.

33. parce: "Stop, leave off (from)" + dative (*mentiendo* [< *mentire*], below). *in verba ista* is explained as periphrasis for a dative with *parcere* that would mean *noli uti*. Hence *parce in verba ista* should mean, "don't use these words," and *parce metiendo* should mean, "stop lying." The whole phrase, then, is grammatically quite odd, a very compressed pair of usages with *parcere*, which (nevertheless) clearly means, "Stop lying with these words."

35   Isto accepto, sititor alioquin novitatis, "Immo vero,"
inquam, "impertite sermonis non quidem curiosum, sed qui
velim scire vel cuncta vel certe plurima. Simul iugi quod
insurgimus aspritudinem fabularum lepida iucunditas
levigabit."

35. alioquin: "in general," or much like the colloquialism "basically." A word that does not appear in Cicero, it was one of Apuleius' favorite particles: he uses it 35 times in the *Metamorphoses*, 5 times in Book 1 alone.

36. impertite sermonis...non curiosum: "share your conversation with one who is not nosey." The intended meaning of this sentence is clear, but the construction is obscure. The commonest construction with this verb is the accusative of the thing shared and the dative of the person with whom it is shared. The MS reading here gives two accusatives, *sermones* (pl.) and *curiosum*. The reading *sermones* requires either understanding a double accusative (not otherwise provable with this verb) or else emending *curiosum*, which was the choice of Heins, who printed *curiosus sum*. Helm prefers to emend *sermones* to *sermonis* (genitive s.): the genitive *sermonis* can be understood as partitive, "(some of) your conversation." Hanson prefers the ablative *sermone*, a construction that Apuleius also used in *Apologia* 97 (*filiam... ne honesto quidem legato impertivit*), so that the construction would be *impertire* + accusative of the person "given to" and ablative of the thing "shared" (as with the verb *donare*).

(me) qui velim: "one who would like to know" (*velim* is present subjunctive, a characteristic clause [shows not the particular person, but the kind of person]).

The theme of the main character's nosiness, or *curiositas*, forms one of the most important unifying themes of the entire work. As his words make clear, and despite his claim to be *non curiosus*, he misses no opportunity to encounter novel or entertaining experiences. While his inquisitiveness here seems harmless, it implies an unhealthy interest and invariably lands him in trouble and is the immediate cause of his transformation into an ass in Book 4. A good overall presentation may be found in Schlam 1992, 48–57. The word *curiositas* itself was rare in Latin before Apuleius either reinvented it or gave it new life.

37. iugi: (genitive < *iugum*, "ridge") goes with *aspritudinem*.

39. levigabit: "will relieve," or "will lighten." This verb is formed from the adjective *levis* and the verbalizing suffix -*igo*. Apuleius maintains consistency of metaphor: the pleasure of tales will render smooth (*levis*) the roughness (*aspritudinem*) of the journey.

40   [3]   At ille qui coeperat, "Ne," inquit, "istud mendacium tam
verum est quam siquis velit dicere magico susurramine amnes
agiles reverti, mare pigrum colligari, ventos inanimes
exspirare, solem inhiberi, lunam despumari, stellas evelli,
diem tolli, noctem teneri."

45   Tunc ego in verba fidentior, "Heus tu," inquam, "qui
sermonem ieceras priorem, ne pigeat te vel taedeat reliqua
pertexere." Et ad alium, "Tu vero crassis auribus et obstinato
corde respuis quae forsitan vere perhibeantur. Minus hercule
calles pravissimis opinionibus ea putari mendacia quae vel

[3]

40. ne here is a strong positive particle, "indeed," a colloquial usage (cf. Greek ναί [nai], "yes").

42. reverti, ...colligari, ...exspirare, ...inhiberi, ...despumare, ...evelli, ...tolli, ...teneri: all infinitives in indirect statement after *velit dicere*. The list of impossibilities is standard witchcraft.

46. ieceras: pluperfect instead of perfect. This is common in Plautus, and Apuleius shows a liking for it.

ne pigeat te...taedeat: hortatory subjunctive (3rd person command). The verbs *pigere* and *taedere* are always impersonal, and are followed by the accusative of the person who performs the verb and an infinitive of a verbal action or the genitive of a noun. So here, "Don't be (too) disgusted or bored...(to)."

47. crassis auribus et obstinato corde respuis: another major theme is opened here, the admonition of the narrator to approach the unbelievable with an open mind instead of "with thick ears and stubborn heart," to suspend disbelief. So our narrator scolds the nameless interlocutor who expresses skepticism and himself immediately adopts an open-minded stance, and thus sets the stage for the first major tale of the work.

48. quae = *ea quae*: "(those) things which."

minus = *non.*

hercule: "by Hercules," a mild oath.

49. calles < *calleo, callēre*. The construction quickly changes to indirect statement, however ("you are not clever [to think]"), rather than complementary infinitives: *ea putari mendacia*, "that those things are considered lies."

50 auditu nova vel visu rudia vel certe supra captum cogitationis
ardua videantur; quae si paulo accuratius exploraris, non
modo compertu evidentia, verum etiam factu facilia senties.
[4] Ego denique vespera, dum polentae caseatae modico secus
offulam grandiorem in convivas aemulus contruncare gestio,
55 mollitie cibi glutinosi faucibus inhaerentis et meacula spiritus
distinentis minimo minus interii. Et tamen Athenis proximo

---

50. auditu...visu: (and *compertu ...factu*) are supines (ablatives of respect), "to hear,...to see" (and "to learn,...to do").

rudia: "new."

supra captum cogitationis: "beyond the grasp of thought" (*captum < captus, captūs*, m., a 4th declension noun).

[4]

51. exploraris = explora(ve)ris

53. denique: "for example," evidently a new meaning established by Apuleius. The narrator now gives an example of a marvel for the veracity of which he vouches personally, to show that tales must be received with an open mind.

vesperā: ablative, "in the evening (yesterday)."

polentae caseatae: "of barley-porridge (flavored with) cheese." The genitive explains *offulam*, "morsel." The diminutive *offula* is characteristic of colloquial speech and is characteristic of Apuleius' style even in non-colloquial-sounding passages.

modico secus: "unusual(ly)," lit., "a little apart," used as an adverb with *grandiorem*.

54. in convivas aemulus: "(as, like) a rival against my guests." Normally, *aemulus* is followed by a dative.

contruncare: properly means "to chop into pieces," but is sometimes used by Plautus (as here) in the sense of "gobble down."

55. mollitie: ablative of cause < *mollities* (5th declension), "because of the softness."

glutinosi: genitive < *glutinosus*, "gluey." *cibi glutinosi* is described by *inhaerentis* and *distinentis*.

meacula: (object of *distintentis*) < *meaculum, meaculi*, n. (and ultimately from the verb *meāre*), "passages."

56. minimo minus interii: "by the smallest margin I did not die."

proximo: "recently."

et ante Poecilen porticum isto gemino obtutu circulatorem aspexi equestrem spatham praeacutam mucrone infesto devorasse, ac mox eundem invitamento exiguae stipis 60 venatoriam lanceam, qua parte minatur exitium, in ima viscera condidisse. Et ecce pone lanceae ferrum, qua bacillum inversi teli ad occipitium per ingluviem subit, puer in mollitiem

57. ante Poecilem porticum: "in front of the Stoa Poikile," a colorful portico in the civic center of Athens. Because it was here that Zeno the philosopher did his teaching, his followers became known as "Stoics." Perhaps Lucius is telling us that his reason for being in Athens was to attend the Stoic philosophical school, a possible allusion to Stoic influence on Apuleius himself.

isto gemino obtutu: "with this very double gaze" (i.e., with my own eyes): *isto* is used for emphasis; Apuleius is not reluctant to use it to refer to the first person (see Book 2.14, *sub istis oculis*).

circulatorem...devorasse,...eundem...condidisse: indirect statement after *aspexi*. But the tenses of the verbs (perfect instead of present) are unusual and seem to have no special force.

58. equestrem spatham: "cavalryman's sword," direct object of *devorasse*.

Scobie's comment (85–86) on the tale of the sword-swallower is helpful: "By giving an account of a *miraculum* that is physically possible, Apuleius prepares the reader for the acceptance of *miracula*

performed by the witches in Aristomenes' [forthcoming] story....Thus the reader is *gradually* introduced into the atmosphere of magic."

59. invitamento exiguae stipis: "at the inducement of a tiny donation."

60. qua parte minatur exitium: "at the point where destruction is threatened," a roundabout way of saying "the business end."

61. pone: "behind," a rare preposition (+accusative).

qua (parte): "where."

inversi teli: "of the upturned spear."

62. occipitium: "(back of the) head."

ingluviem: "throat, gullet."

subit: "goes up from under," a very precise verb here. The subject is *bacillum*, "stick, shaft," a diminutive of *baculum*. The diminutive does not refer to size, but indicates the emotional tone of the speaker.

in mollitiem decorus: "beautiful to the point of effeminacy."

decorus insurgit, inque flexibus tortuosis enervam et exossam
saltationem explicat, cum omnium qui aderamus admiratione.

65 Diceres dei medici baculo, quod ramulis semiamputatis
nodosum gerit, serpentem generosum lubricis amplexibus
inhaerere. Sed iam cedo tu sodes, qui coeperas, fabulam remetire. Ego tibi solus haec pro isto credam, et quod ingressui
primum fuerit stabulum prandio participabo. Haec tibi

70 merces deposita est."

---

63. enervam et exossam saltatio-nem: "a muscle-less and boneless dance."

64. cum...admiratione: we would say, "*to* the astonishment."

65. diceres: "You would say" (apo-dosis of a present unreal condition with protasis unexpressed), followed of course by indirect statement (*serpentem... inhaerere*).

dei medici baculo: "on the scepter of the medicine god" (Aesculapius, in Latin).

quod...nodosum gerit: "the knotty one that he carries."

ramulis semiamputatis nodosum: "knotty with half-cut branches." (*ramulis semiamputatis nodosum* properly belong with *baculo* but are attracted into the relative clause, so that *nodosum* agrees with *baculum*).

67. cedo...sodes: "C'mon,...please," both old words (*cĕdo*, lit., "give"; *sodes*

=*si audes*) found in all kinds of conver-sational Latin. *cedo*, formed from an archaic imperative *do* (from *dare*) and the demonstrative particle *ce* (as in *ecce*). *remetire* is also (deponent) imperative < *remetior*.

68. ego...pro isto credam: "instead of *him*, I shall believe."

quod ingressui primum fuerit stabulum: "the first stopping-place there is (lit., will have been) for the journey." *quod...primum...stabulum = in eo stabulo quod primum*. A *stabulum* was originally a place to quarter animals ("stable"), then by extension included the place where a stable was to be found ("inn") along with the stable, and ulti-mately could refer to the inn alone (*cau-pona, deversorium*).

69. prandio participabo: "I shall share my lunch." *prandio* is ablative, perhaps ablative of respect; *participabo* = "I shall make you a *particeps*."

[5]   At ille: "Istud quidem quod polliceris aequi bonique facio, verum quod incohaveram porro exordiar. Sed tibi prius deierabo solem istum omnividentem deum me vera ac comperta memorare; nec vos ulterius dubitabitis, si Thessaliam proximam

75   civitatem perveneritis, quod ibidem passim per ora populi sermo iactetur quae palam gesta sunt. Sed ut prius noritis

[5]

The Tale of Aristomenes (5–20). This is the first tale in a work that is organized around a series of tales, and as such is especially important in terms of seeing the author's approach to telling stories, listening to stories, and understanding stories. Aristomenes' tale introduces several threads that run throughout the entire *Metamorphoses*, such as magic and witchcraft, and the presence of wondrous events in ordinary human life.

Aristomenes meets Socrates and hears of his misfortunes (5–7). One of the strangers, whose name we find to be Aristomenes, describes his chance meeting with an old friend named Socrates. Appalled by Socrates' appearance, Aristomenes tries to help Socrates recover, and asks what has happened. Socrates explains that he had been beaten and robbed on the road; he was taken in by a woman named Meroë, whose initial kindness quickly became a misfortune.

71. aequi bonique facio: "I regard as fair and good." *aequi* and *boni* are genitives of value.

72. quod incohaveram...exordiar: "I shall give a proper beginning to what

I had started" (an *exordium* was the formal beginning to a speech or a narrative).

tibi...deierabo: "to you (singular) I shall swear an oath." *solem = per solem.*

73.   vera...comperta: "true discoveries."

74. nec vos ulterius dubitabitis: "and you (plural) will no longer doubt."

Thessaliam proximam civitatem: there would normally be a preposition here, probably *ad*, since Thessalia is the name of a territory, not the name of a city. *Thessaliam* and *civitatem* are either in apposition or *Thessaliam* is an adjective ("Thessalian").

75. per ora populi: "on the mouths of the folk." Apuleius often uses *populus* and *populi* (pl.) as equivalents to *homines*.

76. iactetur: the subjunctive is normal in a statement of alleged cause. *sermo* is the subject, "the story is vaunted."

noritis = *no(ve)ritis*: a contracted perfect subjunctive, purpose clause. *Novi* in the perfect is synonymous with *scio* in the present.

cuiatis sim, qui sim: Aegiensis. Audite et quo quaestu me teneam: melle vel caseo et huiusce modi cauponarum mercibus per Thessaliam Aetoliam Boeotiam ultro citro

80   discurrens. Comperto itaque Hypatae, quae civitas cunctae Thessaliae antepollet, caseum recens et sciti saporis admodum commodo pretio distrahi, festinus adcucurri id omne praestinaturus. Sed ut fieri adsolet, sinistro pede

---

77. cuiatis < *cuias*: "from what country?" Similarly formed Latin words are *optimas* (> *optimates*), *Arpinas* ("from Arpinum"), and *nostras* ("our countryman").

qui sim: "(and) who I am." This clause is often deleted by editors on the grounds that it is awkward and redundant, and Aristomenes does not actually answer the question with his name (see next note).

Aegiensis: "a man from Aegium," a town on the north coast of the Peloponnesus, on the Gulf of Corinth. The speaker Aristomenes does not get around to telling us his name until another character in his tale refers to him in 1.6 (line 101), below. For this reason, some editors add *Aristomenes (sum)* here before *Aegiensis* or delete *qui sim*.

quo quaestu me teneam: "with what business I keep myself, what my trade is."

78. cauponarum mercibus: "with tavern merchandise."

80. comperto: "(It) having been learned" a one word ablative absolute, = "when I found out."

itaque is usually first in a sentence in Classical Latin, but Apuleius uses it first only once in 24 occurrences.

Hypatae: locative, "in Hypata," a tiny village near Mt. Oeta.

cunctae Thessaliae antepollet: "excelled all Thessaly." Hypata was in fact of modest importance at some periods as an agricultural market (Scobie 91). The verb *antepollere* is unique to Apuleius; here he uses it with the dative.

81. sciti (< *scitus*) **saporis**: "of fine taste," a genitive of quality. The genitive functions like a second adjective.

82. distrahi: infinitive in indirect statement (the subject is *caseum*), "was being sold in parcels."

adcucurri: more usual with compounds is not to re-duplicate (*accurri*).

id omne praestinaturus: "intending to reserve all of it." *praestinare* is often used simply as a synonym for *emere*, and that may be its meaning here, though the specialized meaning is not excluded. The use here of the future participle to show purpose is perhaps a Grecism, but it is common in all eras of Latin.

83. adsolet = *solet*.

85

profectum me spes compendii frustrata est. Omne enim pridie
Lupus negotiator magnarius coemerat. Ergo igitur inefficaci
celeritate fatigatus, commodum vespera oriente, ad balneas
processeram.

[6] Ecce Socraten contubernalem meum conspicio. Humi
sedebat scissili palliastro semiamictus, paene alius lurore, ad
90
miseram maciem deformatus, qualia solent Fortunae
decermina stipes in triviis erogare. Hunc talem, quamquam
necessarium et summe cognitum, tamen dubia mente propius

84. omne: "the whole batch" (direct object of *coemerat*).

85. Lupus negotiator magnarius: "Mr. Wolf the wholesale merchant," a comic but appropriate name. From Aristomenes' point of view, "Lupus" illustrates the man's greed, but of course Aristomenes had intended to do the same thing himself. The significance of names in Apuleius is treated in detail by B. Hijmans in Hijmans, B. Jr., and van der Paart, R., *Aspects of Apuleius' Golden Ass,* Groningen 1978, pp. 107–122.

ergo igitur: a typical conversational redundancy of which Apuleius is fond, "Therefore for that reason."

86. commodum here is an adverb, "just (as)." This is one of Apuleius's favorite words.

vespera oriente: "(as) the evening (star was) rising", ablative absolute.

87. processeram: pluperfect for perfect.

[6]

88. Socraten: a Greek accusative. The Socrates portrayed here is very different from his Platonic namesake. The use of his name perhaps serves to invoke Socratic values on the surface of the narrative at the same time that they are ignored by the characters in the tale.

89. scissili (< *scissilis, -e,* 3rd declension), "torn." *palliastro* (< *palliastrum,*

-tri, n.), "cheap cloak." These two words are not found prior to Apuleius.

semiamictus: "half-clothed."

paene alius: "almost someone else."

90. qualia...decermina: "like those cast-offs who..."

91. hunc talem: "The way he was, ..."

accessi. 'Hem,' inquam 'mi Socrates, quid istud? Quae facies!
Quod flagitium! At vero domi tuae iam defletus et conclamatus

95   es, liberis tuis tutores iuridici provincialis decreto dati, uxor
persolutis inferialibus officiis luctu et maerore diuturno
deformata, diffletis paene ad extremam captivitatem oculis
suis, domus infortunium novarum nuptiarum gaudiis a
suis sibi parentibus hilarare compellitur. At tu hic larvale

100   simulacrum cum summo dedecore nostro viseris.'

---

93. quae facies! "what an appearance!" (*facies, faciei*, f., 5th declension).

94. iam defletus et conclamatus es: "you have already been mourned and proclaimed as dead."

95. tutores...dati: "guardians have been assigned." In Roman Law, a minor had to have a guardian (*tutor*) if all his direct male ancestors were dead, usually one of his father's brothers, or one of his father's brothers' sons, if there were any. If none of these near kinsmen (called "agnates") was alive (as, evidently, here), then the Praetor (in Rome) or the chief magistrate (in a province) would assign a guardian, usually from the clan (*gens*).

iuridici provincialis decreto: "by the decree of the provincial magistrate." These *iuridici* (though they do not seem to have been called *provinciales*) were first appointed for Italy outside Rome under Hadrian and are also known for Egypt; they may have been discontinued under Macrinus (in 217 or 218). This is all consistent with the known dates of Apuleius' life. It is otherwise possible to make too much of the use of the title here; the character is perhaps exaggerating his shock at the appearance of his friend, and using terminology that is somewhat inappropriate for the province of Achaea.

96. inferialibus officiis: "funeral services." The text of *inferialibus* is disputed, other candidates being *ferialibus* and *feralibus*; but they all come to the same thing.

uxor here is the subject of *compellitur* after the participle (*deformata*) and two ablative absolutes (*persolutis...officiis, diffletis...oculis*).

97. diffletis...oculis suis: ablative absolute, "her eyes...wept out."

ad extremam captivitatem: "to the final point of enslavement," i.e., blindness.

98. domus (genitive) **infortunium...hilarare compellitur:** "is being pressured to gladden the misfortune of the house."

a suis sibi parentibus: the collocation *suis sibi* is redundant and colloquial, and common in Apuleius as well as in Roman comedy.

99. larvale simulacrum: "looking like a ghost." (Lit., "a ghostly image." Grammatically, *simulacrum* is in apposition to *tu*.)

100. cum summo dedecore nostro: "to our very great disgrace."

" 'Aristomene,' inquit, 'ne tu fortunarum lubricas ambages et instabiles incursiones et reciprocas vicissitudines ignoras.' Et cum dicto sutili centunculo faciem suam iam dudum punicantem prae pudore obtexit ita ut ab umbilico pube tenus

105   cetera corporis renudaret. Nec denique perpessus ego tam miserum aerumnae spectaculum, iniecta manu ut adsurgat enitor.

[7]   "At ille, ut erat, capite velato, 'Sine, sine,' inquit, 'fruatur diutius tropaeo Fortuna quod fixit ipsa.'

---

101.   Aristomene: vocative. Aristomenes' name means something like "valorous strength."

ne: as above (1.3, line 40) "indeed."

103. et cum dicto: a favorite phrase of Apuleius (perhaps his own invention) and the equivalent of *nec mora* (Kenney): "and no sooner had [he] spoken." Lit., "together with the word."

sutili centunculo: "with his stitched rag cloak." (*centunculum* is diminutive of *cento*, a garment made of stitched-together rags.)

faciem...punicantem: "his blushing face" (*punicare* is lit., "to dye with red," but the word is not found before Apuleius).

104. ita ut calls attention to the upcoming result clause.

pube tenus: "as far as his groin" (*tenus* + ablative is a post-positive preposition [always *follows* its noun]).

105. cetera corporis: "the rest of (the parts of) his body" (same construction as *ardua montium*, etc., in 1.2 [line 21], above).

denique = *igitur:* according to Scobie, Apuleius uses the word in this sense about 30 times.

perpessus (sum) < *perpetior.*

[7]

108. sine, sine: a rhetorical repetition, like "Stop, stop."

fruatur: "let...enjoy," subjunctive after *sine* with omission of *ut. fruor* takes the ablative.

110 "Effeci sequatur, et simul unam e duabus laciniis meis
exuo eumque propere vestio dicam an contego, et ilico lavacro
trado. Quod unctui, quod tersui, ipse praeministro; sordium
enormem eluviem operose effrico; probe curato, ad hospitium,
lassus ipse, fatigatum aegerrime sustinens perduco. Lectulo
115 refoveo, cibo satio, poculo mitigo, fabulis permulceo. Iam
adlubentia proclivis est sermonis et ioci et scitum etiam
cavillum, iam dicacitas intimida, cum ille imo de pectore
cruciabilem suspiritum ducens, dextra saeviente frontem

110. sequatur = *ut sequatur*, result clause used as the object of *effeci*, hence a so-called "substantive result clause," sometimes a "jussive noun clause" ("jussive" because of the implied command in the introductory verb). The use of the present instead of the imperfect subjunctive is unusual; Scobie suggests this was on analogy of verbs like *novi* (a true present perfect).

laciniis (< *lacinia, -ae*, f.), "garments," the usual meaning in the plural. The singular means "hem" or "fringe" (see 1.23 [line 440], below).

111. dicam an contego: "or (perhaps) I should say, I covered him."

lavacro: "to the public bath."

112. quod: "What (was needed for)."

tersui: dative (4th declension) of *tersus < tergēre.*

praeministro: "do (as a service) before (being asked)."

sordium: genitive pl. of *sordes*

113. curato: a one-word ablative absolute, "when this had been taken care of."

ad hospitium = *ad tabernam.*

114. fatigatum: i.e., *eum fatigatum*, direct object in effect of both *sustinens* and *perduco* ("holding him up,...I led him").

lectulo...cibo...poculo...fabulis: ablatives of means.

116. adlubentia: "willingness, desire (for)" + genitive. This word occurs first in Apuleius.

ioci is nominative pl., parallel to *adlubentia, cavillum*, and *dicacitas*. The verb is *est* (*adlubentia proclivis est*), which agrees with its closest subject.

etiam: the reading is Helm's emendation, since the intensive use of *et* ("even") in a sequence of connective uses of *et* seems harsh.

117. intimida: "fearless." An emendation by Helm of *timida* ("shy"); editors who have felt uncomfortable with *timida* have also suggested *tumida* ("pompous") or *tinnula* ("jangling"). The idea is that Aristomenes engaged Socrates in the kind of sharp banter common between good friends.

cum: ("when") *ille...ducens, ...replaudens, ...infit.*

replaudens, 'Me miserum,' infit, 'qui dum voluptatem
120 gladiatorii spectaculi satis famigerabilis consector, in has
aerumnas incidi. Nam, ut scis optime, secundum quaestum
Macedoniam profectus, dum mense decimo ibidem attentus
nummatior revortor, modico prius quam Larissam accederem,
per transitum spectaculum obiturus, in quadam avia et
125 lacunosa convalli a vastissimis latronibus obsessus atque
omnibus privatus tandem evado. Et utpote ultime adfectus

119. replaudens: "smacking again and again."

qui dum: "because while I ...": note that *qui* is the subject of a first person singular verb.

120. famigerabilis: "well known, famous." A colorful compound formed from *fam(a)* ("fame") + *-ger* ("bringer, holder") + *-abilis* ("-able"). Apuleius liked the word, which he used four times in the *Metamorphoses*; previously it is found only in Varro (*LL* 6.55). It could be an archaism, or a reinvention by Apuleius.

121. secundum quaestum: "in accordance with (my) business." *secundum* (+ accusative) is the preposition.

122. Macedoniam: accusative of motion, unusual with names of countries. Apuleius used this same construction above in 1.5, line 74 (*Thessaliam civitatem*).

mense decimo should strictly be taken with *revortor*, "I returned in the tenth month," which probably means "after nine months." The phrase also goes loosely with the immediately following participle (*attentus*), which would normally need an accusative of duration. This mixing of the temporal accusative and temporal ablative is not unusual in all periods of Latin.

ibidem attentus: "having been kept busy there."

123. nummatior: "somewhat wealthier."

modico: "a bit."

124. per transitum spectaculum obiturus: "intending to take in the show on my way by," future participle to show purpose (see above, 1.5 [line 83]: *praestinaturus*).

126. omnibus: ablative of separation with *privatus*, "deprived of everything."

utpote ultime adfectus: "inasmuch as I was desperately shaken" (*utpote* indicates that its clause or phrase is causal).

ad quandam cauponam Meroen, anum sed admodum scitulam, devorto, eique causas et peregrinationis diuturnae et domuitionis anxiae et spoliationis [diuturnae et dum]

130   miserae refero. Quae me nimis quam humane tractare adorta, cenae gratae atque gratuitae ac mox, urigine percita, cubili suo adplicat. Et statim miser, ut cum illa adquievi, ab unico congressu annosam ac pestilentem servitutem contraho; et

127. cauponam Meroen: "innkeeper named Meroë." The usual word for female innkeeper is *copa*. Her name is trisyllabic (me-ro-e) and suggests *merum* ("unmixed wine") in Latin, but it is also the name of an island in the Nile River where there was a temple of Isis. Both suggestions are probably intended by Apuleius.

anum sed admodum scitulam: "old but quite cute."

128. et...et...et: "not only (of)..., but also (of)..., and (of)..."

129. domuitionis is an old word formed from *domum* + *itio*, a "going home."

[diuturnae et dum]: these words are a copyist's mistake and should not be translated. Normally, I have omitted or changed obvious errors, but this illustrates in a particularly clear way how a copyist can glance at the previous line, where he would have seen **diuturnae et domuitionis** and misread it for *diuturnae et dum*. This kind of error is called "dittography."

130. quae = *et ea*: "And she," an example of "linking *Qui*."

me is the direct object first of *tractare*, but then also of *applicat*.

nimis quam humane: "really quite decently."

131. gratae atque gratuitae: used for the alliteration and the word-play on the meanings. The use of one word to explain, imply, or reflect the meaning of another is called figura etymologica.

(me) cenae (dative)**...ac mox... cubili suo applicat:** "she led me to dinner and soon to bed."

urigine percita: "stirred by passion." *percită* (< *perceo*) is probably nominative (i.e., this is not an ablative absolute). Alternatively, the ablative absolute, "with passion stirred up" (*urigine percitā*) would have the same sense. *urigo* (*uriginis*, f.) is ultimately < *urere*, "burn." It is stronger than *lubido*, and is first found in Apuleius.

132. ut: "when." *cum* is the preposition, governing *illā*.

133. servitutem is Helm's conjecture for the meaningless *cum* (or *con-*) of the MSS (the reading is actually the abbreviation c̄). It seems that the scribe began to write *contraho* and somehow omitted a word. Helm's reading ignores the corrupt text and is based simply on the sense of the passage, a method also adopted by others; thus *cladem* ("disaster," another suggestion by Helm, adopted in his third edition), or *noxam* (Giarratano). Others have tried to retain *con-* as a prefix, such

ipsas etiam lacinias quas boni latrones contegendo mihi
135   concesserant in eam contuli, operulas etiam quas adhuc
vegetus saccariam faciens merebam, quoad me ad istam
faciem quam paulo ante vidisti, bona uxor et mala Fortuna
perduxit.'

[8] " 'Pol quidem tu dignus,' inquam, 'es extrema sustinere,
140   si quid est tamen novissimo extremius, qui voluptatem
Veneriam et scortum scorteum Lari et liberis praetulisti.'

---

as with *coniunctionem* ("association," Chodaczek), *contagionem* ("disease," keeping it a metaphor with the verb *contraho*, Lütjohann and Kronenberg). No solution has satisfied everyone.

134. boni latrones is ironic. Apuleius' characters frequently use the word *bonus* for irony (the robbers are evil, not good) or as a euphemism (such as when describing witches, so as not to speak ill of them).

contegendo mihi: gerundive (in the dative, showing purpose), "for covering myself." This use of the gerundive is rare.

135. operulas: "wages."

adhuc vegetus: "while I was still vigorous."

136. saccariam faciens: "working as a sack-carrier."

137. bona uxor: again ironic, or perhaps, since Meroë turns out to be a witch, Aristomenes is being euphemistic: *uxor* is a generous label in any case.

[8]

Socrates explains that he has been cursed by a witch (8–10). In response to Lucius' low opinion of Meroë, Socrates shows great fear, and explains that in fact Meroë is a witch, who terrorized and eventually transported a whole town to a remote mountain. Socrates has been on the run from Meroë.

139. Pol: "by Pollux," a mild oath, shortened for "*edepol.*" Men swore by Pollux, women by Castor (*mecastor*).

140. (si quid)...novissimo extremius: "(anything)...more extreme than (your) most recent (condition)." "Most recent" or "last" is the usual meaning of forms of *novissimus. extrema...extremius* is another example of polyptoton (see note on *felices... felicioribus* in 1.1 [line 8], above).

voluptatem Veneriam et scortum scorteum Lari et liberis: a particularly exuberant series of alliterations.

141. scortum scorteum: "leathery whore" (*scorteus*, "made of leather"), a phrase employed strictly for the alliterative pun, since Aristomenes himself had never seen the woman. According to Varro (*LL*

"At ille, digitum a pollice proximum ori suo admovens et in stuporem attonitus, 'Tace, tace,' inquit; et circumspiciens tutamenta sermonis, 'Parce,' inquit, 'in feminam divinam,

145   ne quam tibi lingua intemperante noxam contrahas.'

" 'Ain tandem?' inquam. 'Potens illa et regina caupona quid mulieris est?'

" 'Saga,' inquit, 'et divina, potens caelum deponere, terram suspendere, fontes durare, montes diluere, manes sublimare,

150   deos infimare, sidera exstinguere, Tartarum ipsum illuminare.'

7.84), the word *scortum* originally meant "(animal) skin" or "hide."

Lari et liberis: "to your home and children," lit., "to your Lar (household god) and children."

143. circumspiciens tutamenta sermonis: "checking out the safety of the conversation."

144. parce: "Stop."

in feminam divinam presumes a verb like (*ut*) *dicas*, or *dicere* to follow *parce*; classical Latin would have a dative here.

145. ne quam...noxam contrahas: "lest you incur any damage" (*quam = aliquam*, as always after *si, nisi, num,* and *ne*). A negative clause of purpose.

146. ain tandem: "Oh, really?" *Ain = ais-ne* (< *aio*, "so say you?") and *tandem* expresses impatience.

147. quid mulieris: "what (kind) of woman?"

148. saga: "a witch." The theme of witchcraft is here introduced in the tale of Aristomenes. This theme, or perhaps better, in view of Apuleius's promise to stitch together tales, thread, permeates the entire work. Later it will be Lucius' insatiable curiosity about witchcraft that causes him to be turned into an ass.

divina, potens: (*potens* goes on to govern the infinitives which follow, see next note). *divina potens* (which Helm retains) is Colvius's emendation for the MSS *divini potens* ("with the power of a god"). Since the phrase *saga illa et divini potens* occurs in Book 9 (ch. 29), it is now usual not to change *divini* to *divina,* in which case one would omit the comma between this word and *potens.* Aristomenes has asked, "*potens illa?*" and Socrates replies directly, "*saga et divini potens.*"

potens...deponere,...suspendere,... durare, etc.: "able to pull down,...to raise up,...to harden," etc.

" 'Oro te,' inquam, 'aulaeum tragicum dimoveto et siparium scaenicum complicato et cedo verbis communibus.'

" 'Vis,' inquit, 'unum vel alterum, immo plurima eius audire facta? Nam ut se ament efflictim non modo incolae,

155 verum etiam Indi vel Aethiopes utrique vel ipsi Anticthones, folia sunt artis et nugae merae. Sed quod in conspectum plurium perpetravit, audi.

[9] " 'Amatorem suum, quod in aliam temerasset, unico verbo mutavit in feram castorem, quod ea bestia, captivitati metuens

160 ab insequentibus se praecisione genitalium liberat, ut illi

151. dimoveto: future imperative, "take away."

152. cedo: "Give (it to me)," as in 1.4 [line 67], above.

verbis communibus: ablative of means, "in ordinary words."

154. ut se ament...non modo incolae: "that not only local inhabitants love her." A verb like *efficit*, "she causes (that)" is implied. (The use of *se* instead of *eam* or *ipsam* is a colloquialism, analogous to the indirect reflexive, going back not to its own verb but the governing verb, which here is only the implied [!] *efficit*.)

155. Aethiopes utrique: "both (kinds of) Ethiopians," i.e., those who lived both east and west of the Nile River.

ipsi Antichthones: "the very men on the other side of the earth," a tribe of legend.

156. folia sunt artis: "are (mere) leaves of her art," i.e., very light pieces, like feathers. Molt cites Cicero *Att.* 8.5: *pluma et folio facilius moveri*, "easier to move than a feather or leaf."

[9]

158. temerasset = *temera(vi)sset*: (pluperfect subjunctive, again because of the alleged cause), "had made a (rash) advance (upon)." *temerare* + *in* + accusative does not occur elsewhere.

159. captivitati metuens: the dative after *metuo* is not found elsewhere.

160. se praecisione genitalium liberat: "frees itself by chewing off its genitals." This interesting myth was common in antiquity; Servius, the scholiast on Vergil (*Georgics* 1.58), connects the word *castor* to *castrare*.

ut illi quoque simile...proveniret: "so that a similar thing would befall him also." *illi* is dative ("to him"), *simile* is nominative, s., n.

quoque simile, quod venerem habuit in aliam, proveniret. Cauponem quoque vicinum atque ob id aemulum deformavit in ranam, et nunc senex ille dolio innatans vini sui adventores pristinos in faece submissus officiosis roncis raucus appellat.

165 Alium de foro, quod adversus eam locutus esset, in arietem deformavit, et nunc aries ille causas agit. Eadem amatoris sui uxorem, quod in eam dicacule probrum dixerat, iam in sarcina praegnationis obsepto utero et repigrato fetu perpetua praegnatione damnavit et, ut cuncti numerant, iam octo

---

161. quod venerem habuit in aliam: "because he had sex with another." This is a common metonymy for Venus's name.

162. atque ob id aemulum: *aemulum* is accusative singular masculine, "and a rival." *ob id* draws the conclusion from the previous noun (*cauponem vicinum*), "for this reason."

163. dolio innatans vini sui: "swimming in a vat of his own wine." *dolio* is ablative of location (more commonly with *in*).

164. officiosis roncis: "with dutiful croaks." The combination *roncis raucus* is an example of onomatopoeia.

raucus: "in a hoarse voice."

166. aries...agit: an ancient lawyer joke. *Aries* was often used as a term of abuse for *causidici*, evidently because of their alleged love of fighting.

eadem: forms of *idem* ("the same") are often used at the beginnings of sentences or long clauses to reinforce the continuation of the noun from the previous sentence, with no particular emphasis being placed on the "sameness" of the noun. So here, translate simply, "She also..."

167. uxorem is the direct object of *damnavit*, after several interruptions.

iam in sarcina praegnationis: "already in the baggage of pregnancy."

168. obsepto utero et repigrato fetu: ablative absolute, "with her womb sewn shut and the baby held back." The verb *repigrare* is not found before Apuleius.

perpetuā praegnatione damnavit: "condemned her to unending pregnancy."

169. iam octo annorum onere... distenditur: a good example of the use of the present tense in Latin (frequently in combination with *iam*) to show continuation over time, where English uses the present perfect. Thus, translate, "she *has been* swollen...with a burden of eight years."

170   annorum onere misella illa velut elephantum paritura
distenditur.

[10]   " 'Quae cum subinde faceret ac multi nocerentur,
publicitus indignatio percrebruit statutumque ut in eam die
altera severissime saxorum iaculationibus vindicaretur.
175   Quod consilium virtutibus cantionum antevortit, et, ut illa
Medea unius dieculae a Creone impetratis indutiis totam eius
domum filiamque cum ipso sene flammis coronalibus

---

170. velut elephantum paritura: "as if she were going to give birth to an elephant," speaking presumably also of size, not just of time. Plautus (*Stichus* 168) calls the usual pregnancy of an elephant ten years.

[10]

172. quae cum subinde faceret ac multi nocerentur: "when she kept doing these things and harming many." The MSS read *quae cum subinde ac multi nocerentur*, a very difficult clause without a verb after *subinde*. Most editors presume that a verb like *fierent* ("kept happening") is missing between *subinde* and *ac*. Helm has supplied *faceret*, "she kept doing," understanding *quae* as accusative ("these things"). Armini suggested that *subinde ac* was intended to join *quae* (nominative) with *multi*, "when she (the pregnant woman) and many (others) kept being harmed." Other changes have been suggested, such as emending *multi* to *a multis* and the verb to *noscerentur* (or a synonym), and understanding *quae* as nominative n., "these things were discovered by many."

173. publicitus: see line 212, note on *naturalitus*.

statutumque = *statutumque est*: "it was decided."

ut in eam…severissime…vindicaretur: "that the severest punishment should be exacted on her."

174. quod = *et illud*: (linking *Qui*), describing *consilium*.

175. virtutibus cantionum: "by the power (lit., virtues) of her spells. *cantionum < cantio*.

ut illa Medea…sic haec: "just as that famous Medea, … so this woman." The reference is to Euripides' *Medea*, where she gave Jason's bride Creusa a robe and a golden crown as wedding gifts; when Creusa put on the robe and crown, flames burst out, killed Creusa and her father King Creon, and set the palace afire.

176. unius dieculae…impetratis indutiis: "a truce of a single little day having been granted."

177. flammis coronalibus: "with the flames from a crown."

deusserat, sic haec devotionibus sepulcralibus in scrobem procuratis, ut mihi temulenta narravit proxime, cunctos in

180   suis sibi domibus tacita numinum violentia clausit, ut toto biduo non claustra perfringi, non fores evelli, non denique parietes ipsi quiverint perforari, quoad mutua hortatione consone clamitarent quam sanctissime deierantes sese neque ei manus admolituros et, si quis aliud cogitarit, salutare

185   laturos subsidium. Et sic illa propitiata totam civitatem

---

178. deusserat < *de+urere* (pluperfect indicative).

devotionibus sepulcralibus in scrobem procuratis: ablative absolute, "invocations of the dead having been carried out into a ditch." *Devotio* means the making of a solemn vow; *sepulcralibus* defines that vow as made to the dead. The passage vaguely recalls the invocation of the dead by Odysseus at the beginning of *Odyssey* 11.

179. temulenta: "(when she was) a little tipsy."

cunctos...clausit: "she closed everyone up."

in suis sibi domibus: as in 1.6 (line 98: *a suis sibi parentibus*) the collocation *suis sibi* is redundant.

180. tacitā numinum violentiā: "with the silent force of the spirits."

ut: result clause.

toto biduo: ablative, instead of accusative, for duration.

182. mutuā hortatione: "by common pleading."

183. consone clamitarent: "they shouted out as one." The adverb *consone* is not found before this passage.

quam sanctissime deierantes: "swearing the most solemn oaths possible."

sese neque ei manus admolituros (esse) et...laturos: Indirect statement, "(that) they would not raise their hands against her, and...they would bring." *sese = se.*

184. cogitarit: = *cogita(ve)rit*, perfect subjunctive: this primary tense stands for what would have been a present subjunctive in direct speech. *si quis... cogitarit,...laturos* in indirect statement would have been *si quis...cogitet,...ferremus* in direct speech. The condition therefore is a mixed future condition, with an unreal (less vivid) protasis and a real (more vivid) apodosis.

salutare...subsidium: "rescue and help" (lit., rescuing aid).

absolvit. At vero coetus illius auctorem nocte intempesta cum tota domo, id est, parietibus et ipso solo et omni fundamento, ut erat, clausa, ad centesimum lapidem in aliam civitatem, summo vertice montis exasperati sitam et ob id ad aquas
190　sterilem, transtulit. Et quoniam densa inhabitantium aedificia locum novo hospiti non dabant, ante portam proiecta domo discessit.'

[11]" 'Mira,' inquam, 'nec minus saeva, mi Socrates, memoras. Denique mihi quoque non parvam incussisti
195　sollicitudinem, immo vero formidinem, iniecto non scrupulo sed lancea, ne quo numinis ministerio similiter usa sermones

---

186. coetūs illius auctorem: "the man responsible for that meeting": this is the direct object of *transtulit.*

nocte intempestā: "in the dead of night."

188. ut erat, clausā: "as it was, closed up" (from her spell). Assuming the speaker is maintaining strict grammar, *clausā* modifies *domō* and so must be ablative, just like the appositives after *id est* (*parietibus, solo, fundamento*).

ad centesimum lapidem: "near the 100th (mile-)stone" from the city.

189. ad aquas sterilem: "barren with regard to water." The plural (*aquas*) perhaps means "sources of water."

191. locum novo hospiti non dabant: "were not providing space for a new guest."

---

[11]

The witches attack Socrates (11–13). Socrates and Aristomenes go to bed, but Aristomenes cannot sleep. Suddenly the doors burst open and two witches, Panthia and Meroë, cast a curse on Socrates and abuse Aristomenes, who is to be the agent of bringing the curse to its conclusion.

195. iniecto non scrupulo sed lanceā: "since you have inserted not a point but a whole spear": the Latin has a hard-to-capture word-play on *scrupulum* (lit., "a piece of gravel," also "a small weight," "a cause for concern") and *lancea* ("spear"). The verb *inicere* would mean "insert" with *scrupulum*, but with *lancea* one would expect perhaps *traicere* ("pierce").

196. ne quo numinis ministerio similiter usa: "lest, by similarly using some divine aid, (she) ...;" *quo = aliquo* after *ne*; *usa < utor* (+ abl) agrees with *anus.*

istos nostros anus illa cognoscat. Itaque maturius quieti nos reponamus et, somno levata lassitudine, noctis antelucio aufugiamus istinc quam pote longissime.'

200 "Haec adhuc me suadente, insolita vinolentia ac diuturna fatigatione pertentatus bonus Socrates iam sopitus stertebat altius. Ego vero, adducta fore pessulisque firmatis, grabatulo etiam pone cardines supposito et probe adgesto, super eum me recipio. Ac primum prae metu aliquantisper vigilo, dein

205 circa tertiam ferme vigiliam paululum coniveo. Commodum

---

197. maturius: "rather quickly" (comparative adverb).

198. reponamus... aufugiamus: hortatory subjunctives.

noctis antelucio: "at the predaylight of night" (i.e., just before dawn).

200. me suadente: ablative absolute, "as I was urging."

202. adductā fore: ablative absolute, "with the door pulled shut" (*fore*, ablative < *foris*). Scobie (103) suggests that the use of the singular *foris* implies that the "door" to Aristomenes' and Socrates' room consists of a single leaf or panel (*valva*), instead of the pair (*fores*) that was usual. Aristomenes and Socrates are staying in a *hospitium* of poor standard. The *pessuli* would be located at the top and bottom edges. A few lines later, however, Apuleius will refer to *ianuae* (plural).

grabatulo: ablative < *grabatulus*, "cot," a diminutive of *grabatus* (spelled inconsistently with one "t" or two). The basic furnishings in a *cella* of a *taberna*

were a bed (*lectus*, here *grabatus*), a lamp (*lucerna* or *candelabrum*), and a chamberpot (*matella*).

203. pone: the preposition (+ accusative), as above, line 61. The MSS read *cardine*, which Helm has emended to *cardines* (plural), thinking of the bi-valve door; on Scobie's analysis (see above on *adducta fore*), *cardinem* would be more logical; *cardine* would be an easy mistake for a scribe in that case, since *cardinem* would normally have been written *cardinē*. But a few lines below, Apuleius refers to *cardines* (plural).

probe aggesto: "(having been) pushed up tight" against the door.

205. circa tertiam ferme vigiliam: "right about the third watch," i.e., around midnight. The night was divided into four equal parts called *vigiliae*.

commodum: "just," adverbial like *modŏ*, as in 1.5 (line 86), above. Apuleius was fond of this colloquialism, employing the word in this sense 25 times in the *Metamorphoses*.

quieveram et repente impulsu maiore quam ut latrones
crederes ianuae reserantur, immo vero fractis et evolsis
funditus cardinibus prosternuntur. Grabatulus, alioquin
breviculus et uno pede mutilus ac putris, impetus tanti
210   violentia prosternitur; me quoque evolutum atque excussum
humi recidens in inversum cooperit ac tegit.

[12]   "Tunc ego sensi naturalitus quosdam affectus in
contrarium provenire. Nam ut lacrimae saepicule de gaudio
prodeunt, ita et in illo nimio pavore risum nequivi continere,
215   de Aristomene testudo factus. Ac dum in fimum deiectus
obliquo aspectu quid rei sit, grabatuli sollertia munitus,
opperior, video mulieres duas altioris aetatis: lucernam

---

206. maiore quam ut latrones crederes (facere posse): "greater than you would believe robbers (could make)."

208. alioquin: "in general," like our colloquial use of "basically" (above, 1.2 [line 35]).

209. breviculus: diminutive because of size and weight, but also appropriate to the emotional tone of the passage.

211. (me)...in inversum cooperit: "covered me upside down."

[12]

212. sensi: "I realized **how**" (Latin uses indirect statement, "realized that").

naturalitus: adv., "in accordance with nature," a form not found before Apuleius. Adverbs in *-itus* are not uncommon, such as *antiquitus* and *publicitus*.

affectūs is accusative plural.

214. nequivi < *nequeo*: "I was unable."

215. de Aristomene testudo factus: "(inasmuch as) a turtle (had been) created from Aristomenes."

in fimum: "into the dung." This is an emendation of a questionable reading, *infimum* ("down[ward]").

216. quid rei sit: "what was going on," indirect question depending upon the implied question in *opperior*.

grabatuli sollertia: personification, "by the cleverness of the cot."

217. (dum)...opperior: "while I waited (to find out)."

lucernam lucidam: another alliterative figura etymologica (see note on *gratae atque gratuitae*, 1.7 [line 131], above).

lucidam gerebat una, spongiam et nudum gladium altera. Hoc
habitu Socratem bene quietum circumstetere. Infit illa cum

220   gladio, 'Hic est, soror Panthia, carus Endymion, hic Catamitus
meus, qui diebus ac noctibus illusit aetatulam meam, hic qui
meis amoribus subterhabitis non solum me diffamat probris,
verum etiam fugam instruit. At ego scilicet Ulixi astu deserta
vice Calypsonis aeternam solitudinem flebo.' Et porrecta

225   dextera meque Panthiae suae demonstrato, 'At hic bonus,'
inquit, 'consiliator Aristomenes, qui fugae huius auctor fuit
et nunc morti proximus iam humi prostratus grabatulo

219. circumstetere = *circumsteter-unt*: Apuleius' first use of this common contraction of the 3rd person plural in the perfect tense.

illa cum gladio: we find out a bit later that this is Meroë, Socrates' lover. On the name, see above on 1.7 (line 127).

220. soror Panthia: "my sister Panthia." The address as "sister" is appropriate to witches. The name Panthia means "all divine."

Endymion was a hunter for whom the Moon-goddess developed a passion and who therefore put to sleep so that she could embrace him in secret. *Catamitus* is a corrupted Latinized form of the Greek Ganymedes, who was a Trojan youth for whom Zeus developed a passion; Zeus snatched him away to Olympus to be his cupbearer. (The English word "catamite" is an abusive word for homosexual lover.)

221. diebus ac noctibus: ablative instead of accusative for duration.

aetatulam: diminutive < *aetas* ("age"), "youth."

222. meis amoribus subterhabitis: ablative absolute, "disdaining my love."

probris < *probrum*: "with slanders."

223. scilicet indicates that the sentence is sarcastic or ironic.

Ulixi: genitive of *Ulixes*, the Latin form of the name Odysseus. The English "Ulysses" comes from the Latin form.

deserta vice Calypsonis: "abandoned like Calypso"; *deserta* is nominative, *vice* is adverbial. Calypso was the demi-goddess on Ogygia who kept Odysseus on her island for seven years; he finally was able to leave her to return home to his wife Penelope.

225. me...demonstrato: ablative absolute, "pointing me out."

at hic bonus...consiliator Aristomenes: *at* indicates that Meroë, after her short pseudo-tragic lament, is becoming impatient. *bonus consiliator* is ironic.

subcubans iacet et haec omnia conspicit, impune se laturum meas contumelias putat. Faxo eum sero, immo statim, immo

230   vero iam nunc, ut et praecedentis dicacitatis et instantis curiositatis paeniteat.'

[13]   "Haec ego ut accepi, sudore frigido miser perfluo, tremore viscera quatior, ut grabatulus etiam succussu meo inquietus super dorsum meum palpitando saltaret. At bona Panthia, 'Quin

235   igitur,' inquit, 'soror Meroe, hunc primum bacchatim discerpimus vel membris eius destinatis virilia desecamus?'

---

228. impune se laturum (esse) meas contumelias putat: indirect statement, "he thinks (that) he *(se)* will bear my outrages without penalty." *meas contumelias* is ambiguous: Meroë presumably means, "outrages against me," but it could equally mean, "outrages I commit."

The MSS reading here is *impune relaturum*. Editors are uncomfortable with a Latin indirect statement without the subject expressed, so emend to *se laturum* (as here) or *se relaturum* ("that he will report").

229. faxo ut...(paeniteat): "I shall see to it that," an old future perfect <

facio. Like many archaisms, it has a legalistic and formal tone.

eum is the grammatical direct object of the impersonal *paeniteat*, and serves as its notional subject: literally something like "it causes him regret," but simply "he regrets" captures the meaning.

sero, immo statim, immo vero iam nunc: "later – no, pretty soon – no, right now." The acceleration of time reflects Meroë's growing anger.

230. dicacitatis...curiositatis: genitives: the cause for regret with forms of *paenitet* is in the genitive.

[13]

233. viscera quatior: "my insides shook." *viscera* is accusative plural, the accusative of respect ("with respect to my innards") or – since that construction is native to Greek – the "Greek accusative," used especially of body parts. Apuleius uses this construction often.

234. (ut ...) saltaret: "was dancing," another personification of the cot.

235. bacchatim: "in the manner of Bacchants." Bacchants were female worshipers of Dionysus who were reputed to tear animals apart alive as part of their orgiastic celebration of the god. The word *bacchatim* is not found elsewhere.

236. membris...destinatis: "with his limbs tied up."

virilia: n. pl. < *virilis* (3rd declension adj.), "masculine parts, genitals."

"Ad haec Meroe — sic enim reapse nomen eius tunc
fabulis Socratis convenire sentiebam —: 'Immo,' ait, 'supersit
hic saltem qui miselli huius corpus parvo contumulet humo.'

240 Et capite Socratis in alterum dimoto latus, per iugulum
sinistrum capulo tenus gladium totum ei demergit, et sanguinis
eruptionem utriculo admoto excipit diligenter, ut nulla stilla
compareret usquam. Haec ego meis oculis aspexi. Nam etiam,
ne quid demutaret, credo, a victimae religione, immissa

245 dextera per vulnus illud ad viscera penitus cor miseri

**237. nomen...fabulis Socratis con-
venire sentiebam:** "I realized her name
fit with the stories of Socrates."

238. supersit: hortatory subjunctive,
"let this one live."

239. qui (...contumulet): relative
clause of purpose, "so that he...(may
bury)." The word *humo* (< *humus*) is here
masculine; it is usually feminine.

240. capite...dimoto: ablative absolute, "with (his) head moved/turned."

in alterum...latus: "toward the other
side" (*latus < latus, lateris,* n.).

per iugulum sinistrum: "into the
left (side of his) neck."

241. capulo tenus: "up to the
handle."

242. eruptionem...excipit: "caught
the gush."

utriculo admoto: "with (in) a little
leather jug (she had) brought."

243. comparēret = *apparēret*: < *com
+ parēre,* "appeared."

ego meis oculis aspexi: This claim
for the truth of his tale by Aristomenes
reflects the narrator's assertion in 1.4,
above, that he had witnessed the marvel
himself.

**244. ne quid demutaret...a vic-
timae religione:** "so as not to change
anything from the sacrificial ritual." *a
religione victimae* is literally something
like, "from the ritual attention to (objective genitive) a sacrificial victim." Meroë
is portrayed like a Roman haruspex
extracting the entrails (here, heart) of
a sacrificial victim to examine them for
favorable or unfavorable signs.

credo: expresses sarcasm.

245. per vulnus illud: the unusual
word order (instead of *illud vulnus*) may
be used for emphasis; on the other hand,
Apuleius often inverts this word order.

contubernalis mei Meroe bona scrutata protulit, cum ille
impetu teli praesecata gula vocem, immo stridorem incertum,
per vulnus effunderet et spiritum rebulliret. Quod vulnus,
qua maxime patebat, spongia offulciens Panthia, 'Heus tu,'

250   inquit, 'spongia, cave in mari nata per fluvium transeas.' His
editis abeunt et una remoto grabatulo varicus super faciem

---

246. Meroe bona: "the good Meroë,"
another example of a euphemistic expression intended to create a good omen.

scrutata < *scrutor, scrutari:* "having
probed."

cum: "when." This is an example
of the so-called inverted *cum*-clause, "X
was going on ..., when," so that the *cum*-
clause follows rather than precedes the
main idea.

247. praesecatā gulā = *e praesecata
gula,* the ablative reflecting the prefix *ec-*
(*ef-* < *ex*) in *effunderet.*

248. spiritum rebulliret: "was bubbling back his breath."

quod vulnus = *et hoc vulnus* (linking
Qui), direct object of *offulciens.*

249. qua: "where."

spongiā: ablative, "with a sponge."

offulciens < *ob + fulcire:* "stanching."

tu...spongia,...in mari nata: "you,
sponge, born in the sea." Panthia creates
an antithesis between *mari* (sea) and *fluvium* (stream).

250. cave: "be sure (that you)."

his (verbis) editis: "after these
pronouncements."

251. abeunt: Molt (79) explains the
apparent contradiction between this verb
and the continued presence of Meroë
and Panthia by noting that they would
be "leaving" the body of Socrates, but in
getting out of the room they would encounter Aristomenes lying virtually in
the doorway.

unā: adv., "together," with the verb
exonerant.

varicus: adv., "with legs wide apart."

meam residentes vesicam exonerant, quoad me urinae
spurcissimae madore perluerent.

[14]   "Commodum limen evaserant et fores ad pristinum
255   statum integrae resurgunt: cardines ad foramina resident, ad
postes repagula redeunt, ad claustra pessuli recurrunt. At
ego, ut eram, etiam nunc humi proiectus, inanimis, nudus et
frigidus et lotio perlutus, quasi recens utero matris editus,

252. vesicam exonerant: "they unburdened their bladders."

urinae spurcissimae madore: "with the moisture of the filthiest piss." *urina* is not necessarily a polite word in Latin. Urine could be a powerful potion in magical ritual; its value varied by context. In Petronius (*Satyricon* 62.6) a man becomes a wolf after urinating around his clothing (*at ille cicumminxit vestimenta sua, et subito lupus factus est*); Smith takes this as a magical device for protecting the clothing rather than as a cause of the transformation (M. Smith, *Petronius: Cena Trimalchionis*. Oxford: the University Press, 1999, 173; the practice was referred to in a non-technical way a bit earlier, *Satyricon* 57.3.) In any case, the salient point is that the urine here is magical and binding, not merely abusive.

253. perluerent is imperfect subjunctive (secondary sequence) because the previous verbs, while grammatically present tense, are felt as historical presents with meanings equivalent to the perfect.

[14]

Aristomenes tries to escape (14–16). Detecting no signs of life from Socrates, Aristomenes believes that he will be suspected of the murder and tries to escape. He discovers that the exit from the inn is locked and guarded by the door-keeper, who refuses to let him out. Aristomenes despairs of his life and tries to hang himself, but the rope is rotten and breaks.

254. commodum: "just" (see note on 1.5 [line 86] and 1.11 [line 205], above).

et: "when." *commodum...et* works much like *simul...ac*.

255. resident,... redeunt,... recurrunt: the absence of conjunctions (asyndeton) reinforces the speed of the restoration of the door(s). Note that the action is in logical sequence, first the pivots, then the bars, then the locks.

256. repagula: nominative pl. n., "bars" that fit across the door (< *re + pangere*).

258. quasi recens utero matris editus: "as if freshly delivered from my mother's womb."

260 · immo vero semimortuus, verum etiam ipse mihi supervivens
et postumus, vel certe destinatae iam cruci candidatus, 'Quid,'
inquam, 'me fiet, ubi iste iugulatus mane paruerit? Cui
videbor veri similia dicere proferens vera? – "Proclamares
saltem suppetiatum, si resistere vir tantus mulieri nequibas?
Sub oculis tuis homo iugulatur et siles? Cur autem te simile
265 · latrocinium non peremit? Cur saeva crudelitas vel propter

259. verum etiam ipse mihi supervivens et postumus: "indeed, (like) a survivor to myself, and my own posthumous child."

260. cruci candidatus: "candidate for crucifixion." This is a post-classical use of *candidatus*, which formerly referred to the whitened (< *candida*) toga of one running for a magistracy. Those condemned to crucifixion would have been slaves. Hence, the phrase is an amusing oxymoron.

quid...me fiet? "What will become of me?" (Lit., "what will be done with me?") *me* is ablative. (The ablative is explained as instrumental because of the active form of this phrase, as in Plautus, *Aulularia* 776, *tum me faciat quod volt*, "then he may do with me what he wants.")

261. paruerit = *apparuerit*: future perfect indicative. The logic of the Latin is strict: his "appearance" will be in the future but will precede (hence the future perfect) whatever is done to Aristomenes (*fiet*, simple future). The condition is future real (more vivid).

262. proferens: the participle has concessive force, "even while providing..."

proclamares: "wouldn't you call out?" Aristomenes now envisions a series of charges against him by a hypothetical interrogator. The imperfect subjunctive represents the conclusion (apodosis) of a present unreal (or contrary to fact) condition.

263. suppetiatum: supine of purpose, "to bring help" (< *suppetior*).

vir tantus: "big man that you are."

nequibas < *nequeo:* "you were unable." Forms of *possum* in present unreal (contrary to fact) conditions are normally indicative (*poteras* would be used instead of *posses*); so here its negative, *nequibas*, is used instead of *nequeres* in the protasis of the condition.

265. saeva crudelitas: personification, "the savage cruelty," rather than "those savage and cruel perpetrators."

vel propter indicium: "especially on account of the indictment (you could bring)." *vel* (like *et*) often has this intensifying force rather than expressing an alternative.

indicium sceleris arbitro pepercit? Ergo quoniam evasisti mortem, nunc illo redi." '

"Haec identidem mecum replicabam, et nox ibat in diem. Optimum itaque factu visum est anteluculo furtim evadere
270 et viam licet trepido vestigio capessere. Sumo sarcinulam meam, subdita clavi pessulos reduco; at illae probae et fideles ianuae, quae sua sponte reseratae nocte fuerant, vix tandem et aegerrime tunc clavis suae crebra immissione patefiunt.

[15] "Et, 'Heus tu, ubi es?' inquam. 'Valvas stabuli absolve;
275 antelucio volo ire.'

"Ianitor pone stabuli ostium humi cubitans etiam nunc semisomnus, 'Quid? Tu,' inquit, 'ignoras latronibus infestari

266. sceleris arbitro pepercit: "spared (you), a witness of the crime." *pepercit < parco.*

267. illo: adv., "(to) there."

redi: imperative < *red-eo, red-īre.*

268. replicabam: "I was turning (lit., folding) over," a new use of the word, equivalent to the classical *revolvebam.*

269. optimum...factu: "the best (thing)...to do." *factu* is the ablative of the supine form.

anteluculo: ablative, "in the predawn." Not found elsewhere; in 1.11 (line 198), and 1.15 (line 275), below, Apuleius uses *antelucio.*

270. licet: used here as an adverb (modifying *trepido*), "perhaps, although, albeit."

271. reduco: "tried to slide back" (Hanson), as if Apuleius had written *re-ducebam.* The bolts resist, as is clear from the next sentence.

probae et fideles: ironic; also an example of personification, since these are moral, not physical, attributes.

273. clavis suae: genitive, "of their (own) key."

crebra immissione: "with the constant insertion."

patefiunt < *pate-fio, pate-fieri,* passive of *pate-facio.*

[15]

277. latronibus: the ablative without *ab* is explained as ablative of means ("how" the roads are infested) rather than as ablative of (personal) agent.

vias, qui hoc noctis iter incipis? Nam etsi tu alicuius facinoris tibi conscius scilicet mori cupis, nos cucurbitae caput non

280   habemus ut pro te moriamur.'

" 'Non longe,' inquam, 'lux abest. Et praeterea quid viatori de summa pauperie latrones auferre possunt? An ignoras, inepte, nudum nec a decem palaestritis despoliari posse?'

---

278. qui: "you, who" or better, "seeing that you."

hoc noctis: accusative + genitive, "(at) this time of night."

alicuius facinoris tibi conscius: "out of guilt for some crime."

279. scilicet: again, suggests sarcasm or irony, though of course Aristomenes does feel that he might be accused of just this.

mori: infinitive < *morior*, "die."

nos = *ego*.

cucurbitae caput: "melon-head" (lit., "head [made of a] gourd").

280. ut...moriamur: result, "such that I would die." Editors have been puzzled over why the *ianitor* might die if he opens the door. Some have suggested that he is afraid that robbers will break in, others that he is barely awake and is speaking nonsense. Helm agrees with Leo, who asserts that this could not have been spoken by the *ianitor* and should probably be deleted. Scobie plausibly suggests (112) that the *ianitor* is following

up his own vague thought that Aristomenes wants to leave so early to avoid detection for a crime, and that if he lets Aristomenes out he will be convicted in his place.

281. viatori: dative, "*from a traveler*," the so-called dative of separation, a kind of reverse indirect object: one takes something from someone (*auferre*) with the same case with which one gives something to someone (i.e., dative).

282. de summa pauperie: "who is completely impoverished," lit., "of the highest poverty." This use of *de* + ablative instead of a characteristic genitive is postclassical, as is the word *pauperies* (for the classical *paupertas*).

283. nec: "not even."

palaestritis: ablative pl. < *palaestrita, -ae*, m., "wrestling-coaches," i.e., strong, skilled fighters.

despoliari posse: the idea is like that expressed by Juvenal (*Satires* 10.22), who says, *cantabit vacuus coram latrone viator,* "the empty-handed traveler will sing in the face of a robber."

"Ad haec ille marcidus et semisopitus in alterum latus
285   evolutus, 'Unde autem,' inquit, 'scio an convectore illo tuo,
cum quo sero devorteras, iugulato fugae mandes praesidium?'

"Illud horae memini me terra dehiscente ima Tartara inque his canem Cerberum prorsus esurientem mei
prospexisse. Ac recordabar profecto bonam Meroen non
290   misericordia iugulo meo pepercisse, sed saevitia cruci me
reservasse.

---

285. unde...scio an...mandes? "How (lit., from where) do I know whether you entrust": *mandes* is present subjunctive (< *mandare)*, indirect question *(an ...)*.

convectore illo tuo...iugulato: ablative absolute, "with the throat of that fellow-traveler of yours having been cut" or better, "since you have slit the throat of that fellow traveler of yours."

286. sero...devorteras: "you stopped in here late (last night)." The pluperfect again is used for the perfect. *Devortere* (= *devertere*) is just the right verb for stopping at a *deversorium* ("inn"). The spelling with "o" instead of "e" after "v" is common, but Apuleius seems to have been inconsistent (see *deversetur* and *deversatur* in 1.21, line 404, 407, below).

287. illud horae: (accusative + genitive) = *illā horā.*

memini me...prospexisse: indirect statement.

terra dehiscente: ablative absolute.

ima Tartara: accusative pl. n., "the lowest depths of Tartarus" (the Underworld).

288. inque his: "and in them," i.e., in the lowest depths of Tartarus.

Cerberum: Cerberus was the three-headed dog that stood guard at the entrance to the Underworld.

esurientem mei: "hungering for me." *mei* is the genitive of *ego*, here an objective genitive; the construction is explained either as analogous to verbs like *egere* or as an imitation of a Greek construction.

289. Meroen: accusative singular (a Greek form), subject of indirect statement after *recordabar.*

290. pepercisse: perfect infinitive in indirect statement < *parco*, which governs a dative *(iugulo).*

291. reservasse = *reserva(vi)sse.*

[16] "In cubiculum itaque reversus de genere tumultuario mortis mecum deliberabam. Sed cum nullum aliud
telum mortiferum Fortuna quam solum mihi grabatulum
295 sumministraret, 'Iam iam, grabatule,' inquam, 'animo meo
carissime, qui mecum tot aerumnas exanclasti conscius et
arbiter quae nocte gesta sunt, quem solum in meo reatu
testem innocentiae citare possum, tu mihi ad inferos
festinanti sumministra telum salutare.'

[16]

292. de genere tumultuario mortis: "about a hastily-contrived kind of death."

293. deliberabam: a good example of the imperfect in the inceptive sense, "began to ponder."

cum...Fortuna...sumministraret is the main sentence; *telum* is the direct object.

nullum aliud...quam: "no other... than."

295. iam, iam etc.: Aristomenes humorously delivers a melodramatic monologue to his cot.

296. exanclasti = *exancla(vi)sti* (< *exanclare),* "(you) have suffered, gone through." This strange verb is variously explained as from the Greek ἐξαντλεῖν (exantlein), "to sail through," a metaphor from seafaring, or from the same root as *ancilla* (also seen for example in the name of the Roman King, *Ancus* Marcius, "servant of Mars"), so Purser (85). The verb is an archaism that Apuleius liked, employing it eight times in the *Metamorphoses*;

here it adds to the solemn tone of Aristomenes' oration.

conscius et arbiter: "my accomplice and witness (as to)." There is an implicit verb in this phrase, which introduces the next clause.

297. (quae) gesta sunt: "what was done." This is marginally a relative clause, "the things which," and thus an indicative; it could also have been felt as an indirect question, and then in the subjunctive.

quem solum testem...citare possum: "whom alone I can summon as a witness."

298. tu...sumministra: imperative, "you must supply."

mihi... festinanti: dative, "to me... hastening."

299. telum salutare: "the saving weapon" (*salutare* is n. of the adjective *salutaris,* 3rd declension). The phrase is oxymoronic, since Aristomenes wants to use the weapon to kill himself.

300   Et cum dicto restim qua erat intextus aggredior expedire, ac tigillo, quod fenestrae subditum altrinsecus prominebat, iniecta atque obdita parte funiculi et altera firmiter in nodum coacta, ascenso grabatulo ad exitium sublimatus et immisso capite laqueum induo. Sed dum pede altero fulcimentum quo

305   sustinebar repello, ut ponderis deductu restis ad ingluviem astricta spiritus officia discluderet, repente putris alioquin et vetus funis dirumpitur, atque ego de alto recidens Socratem — nam iuxta me iacebat — superruo cumque eo in terram devolvor.

---

300. et cum dicto: a favorite phrase of Apuleius (see 1.6 [line 103], above), "no sooner had I spoken."

quā erat intextus: "(the rope) with which it (the cot) had been tied together."

aggredior expedire: "I stepped up to disentangle."

301. tigillo...iniecta atque obdita parte funiculi: "with (one) part of the rope tossed on and fastened on the (little) beam": *tigillo* is ablative of location.

quod fenestrae subditum: "(the beam) which, flush up under a window." The window is to be viewed as too high or too small to climb out of.

303. sublimatus < *sublimare*: an old (Ennius, Cato) but rare word (found outside Apuleius only in Vitruvius): "raised up." There may be an intentional oxymoron in *sublimatus ad exitium*.

304. fulcimentum: "prop" (accusative).

305. ut...discluderet: purpose clause.

ponderis deductu: "by the pull of (my) weight."

restis...adstricta: (nominative), "the rope, tightened ..."

306. spiritūs officia, "the functions of my breath" (high tragic style).

alioquin: omit in translation; Apuleius often uses this word for color ("in general, basically," see 1.2 [line 35], above) with the first of a pair of adjectives when it seems to have no particular force (Purser xcix). Kenney (210) notes that *alioquin et* has much the same force as the Greek ἄλλως τε καὶ [allōs te kai], which serves to throw emphasis on the second of a pair of words or clauses.

putris...et vetus funis: "rotten old rope" (all nominative). *Vetus (veteris)* is a 3rd declension adjective with only one nominative ending.

310   [17]   "Et ecce in ipso momento ianitor introrumpit, exserte clamitans, 'Ubi es tu, qui alta nocte immodice festinabas et nunc stertis involutus?'

"Ad haec, nescio an casu nostro an illius absono clamore experrectus, Socrates exsurgit prior et 'Non,' inquit, 'immerito
315   stabularios hos omnes hospites detestantur. Nam iste curiosus dum importune irrumpit — credo studio rapiendi aliquid — clamore vasto marcidum alioquin me altissimo somno excussit.'

"Emergo laetus atque alacer insperato gaudio perfusus,
320   et, 'Ecce, ianitor fidelissime, comes [et pater meus] et frater

[17]

Socrates revives, and the two friends leave the inn (17). The door-man bursts into the room and accuses Aristomenes of criminal intent, but Socrates suddenly revives and rebukes the door-keeper. The two friends then depart from the inn.

310. exserte: "at the top of (his) voice." This is the first appearance of this word.

311. altā nocte: "in the dead of night."

312. involutus: "all wrapped up (in your blankets)."

313. nescio an...an: "whether... or."

casu nostro...illius absono clamore: ablatives of cause: "because of my fall... (or) his cacophonous shouts."

314. experrectus < *expergiscor,* deponent verb: the perfect participle is active.

prior: "first" (of two), i.e., before Aristomenes could get up.

315. detestantur: "curse" (> English "detest").

316. importune: "rudely."

credo: once again, indicates sarcasm or irony.

aliquid is accusative, direct object of *rapiendi* (gerund), which is in turn genitive after *studio,* an ablative of cause.

320. comes [et pater meus] et frater meus: Most editors have deleted *et pater meus* as either redundant or absurd (Molt); more recently, the phrase has been accepted as a sign of Aristomenes' exuberance (Scobie, Hanson). It is not clear how old Socrates was intended to be, which some have thought relevant to the question of whether Aristomenes would exuberantly call him *pater.*

meus, quem nocte ebrius occisum a me calumniabaris.' Et cum dicto Socratem deosculabar amplexus.

"At ille, odore alioquin spurcissimi humoris percussus quo me lamiae illae infecerant, vehementer aspernatur. 325 'Apage te,' inquit, 'fetorem extremae latrinae;' et causas coepit huius odoris comiter inquirere.

"At ego miser, adficto ex tempore absurdo ioco, in alium sermonem intentionem eius denuo derivo, et iniecta dextra, 'Quin imus,' inquam, 'et itineris matutini gratiam capimus?' 330 Sumo sarcinulam et, pretio mansionis stabulario persoluto, capessimus viam.

---

321. nocte ebrius: nominative, "(when you were) drunk (last) night."

quem...occisum a me calumniabaris: "who you maliciously claimed had been killed by me." *calumniabaris* is 2nd person s. imperfect deponent < *calumnior*.

323. percussus: "stunned" (< *percutio*).

324. quo me lamiae illae infecerant: "with which those witches had soaked me." Note the (probably) emphatic word order of *lamiae illae*.

325. apage te: "Get away!" (*apage* is Greek, ἄπαγε, equivalent to the Latin verb *abige* < *abigere* < *ab + agere*).

fetorem: "*(you)* stench," in apposition to *te*.

extremae latrinae: genitive, "of the bottom of the latrine."

327. adficto...ioco: ablative absolute, "After making up...a joke."

in alium sermonem: "onto another topic" (lit., another conversation).

328. derivo: "I channel(ed)" as a stream *(-riv-)*.

329. quin imus: "why don't we go?" *imus* < *eo, ire* (irreg.).

gratiam capimus: "get the benefit" (Hanson translates, "take advantage of," a nice turn on the phrase).

330. pretio mansionis persoluto: ablative absolute, "the price of the room having been paid."

stabulario: "to the inn-keeper" (dative).

[18]   "Aliquantum processeramus et iam iubaris exortu cuncta collustrantur. Et ego curiose sedulo arbitrabar iugulum comitis, qua parte gladium delapsum videram; et mecum,
335   'Vesane,' aio, 'qui poculis et vino sepultus extrema somniasti. Ecce Socrates integer, sanus, incolumis. Ubi vulnus, ubi spongia? Ubi postremum cicatrix tam alta, tam recens?' Et ad illum, 'Non,' inquam, 'immerito medici fidi cibo et crapula

[18]

The curse of the witches is fulfilled (18–19). Aristomenes is just beginning to relax from his nervousness over events of the previous night, and Socrates seems to have regained his former composure. They sit near a river to have a meal, and Aristomenes notices that Socrates' color is worsening. When he goes to the river for a drink, Socrates' wound gapes open, the sponge falls out (as foretold in the curse of Meroë), and he finally dies. Aristomenes is then left to bury the body.

332. iubaris exortu: "at the rising of the sun-beams," a poetical turn of phrase.

333. arbitrabar: "I kept examining." *arbitrari* in this sense is consistent with Apuleius' use of *arbiter* (the noun) as "witness" in several passages, but is an unusual sense for the verb (found also in Plautus).

334. qua parte: "at the place where."

gladium delapsum: perhaps indirect statement (*delapsum [esse]*, "that the sword had sunk in"), but perhaps merely a direct object, "the implanted sword."

mecum: "to myself."

335. sepultus < *sepelio, sepelire*: "buried."

somniasti = *somnia(vi)sti* < *somnio, somniare.*

336. integer, sanus, incolumis: the absence of conjunctions is called asyndeton.

338. ad illum...inquam: The use of *ad* + accusative instead of the dative with verbs of saying is Classical and not rare, though it is considered colloquial. So Plautus, for example, has, *ad me magna nuntiavit...gaudia* (*Truculentus* 702), "he reported to me great causes for celebration." The usage was fostered by closely analogous constructs such as, *si ad saxa et ad scopulos haec conqueri ac deplorare vellem*, "if I wanted to lament and deplore these facts to the rocks and the cliffs" (Cicero, *Verres* 5.171), and *ad haec ille subridens* ("chuckling at these things") introducing a quotation in our text just below, and by analogy to verbs like *scribere* (where either the dative or *ad* + accusative is used). Apuleius uses the construction elliptically in Book 3 (ch. 8: *et ad populum talia*, "he [made remarks] like this to the people").

cibo et crapula distentos: "(that) those swollen with food and drink": *distentos* is accusative, subject of indirect statement (the verb is *somniare*).

distentos saeva et gravia somniare autumant. Mihi denique,
340   quod poculis vesperi minus temperavi, nox acerba diras et
truces imagines obtulit, ut adhuc me credam cruore humano
aspersum atque impiatum.'

"Ad haec ille subridens, 'At tu,' inquit, 'non sanguine sed
lotio perfusus es. Verum tamen et ipse per somnium iugulari
345   visus sum mihi. Nam et iugulum istum dolui et cor ipsum
mihi avelli putavi; et nunc etiam spiritu deficior et genua
quatior et gradu titubo et aliquid cibatus refovendo spiritu
desidero.'

---

339. autumant: "(they) maintain, assert."

340. poculis minus temperavi: "I didn't restrain the cups" (*poculis* is dative).

341. ut... credam: result, "such that I believe." The primary tense of *credam* indicates that *obtulit* is a present perfect, "has brought upon me," rather than a simple past.

me...aspersum atque impiatum (esse): indirect statement after *credam*, "that I had been splattered and polluted."

344. lotio < *lotium, lotii*, n.: a colloquialism for *urina*, not necessarily either polite or offensive. Cato uses it in *De Agricultura* 122 and 127 in a clearly neutral tone. Catullus uses both *urina* and *lotium* in offensive contexts in his lampoon of Egnatius (Poem 37.20, *dens...defricatus urina*, and 39.21, *amplius bibisse...loti*).

perfusus < *perfundo*.

per somnium: "during a dream."

ipse...visus sum mihi: lit., "I myself...seemed to myself."

345. iugulum ipsum dolui: accusative of respect (a Greek construction), used especially of body parts, lit., "I hurt with respect to my neck," or "My neck hurt." See also above, note on *viscera quatior* in 1.13 (line 233).

346. spiritu deficior: "I am out of breath" (lit., "I am lacking/weak in breath").

genua: accusative (pl., 4th declension) of respect (see above on *iugulum... dolui*).

347. aliquid cibatūs: "something to eat." *cibatus* is genitive of the whole (from the 4th declension noun *cibatus, -ūs*, m.), qualifying the indefinite quantity *aliquid* (see on *quid sermonis* in 1.2 [line 32], above). The word occurs only in Plautus before this; Apuleius uses the word in the same construction again below, 1.24 (line 466).

refovendo spiritu = *ut spiritus refoveatur* (purpose). *spiritu*, which looks ablative, is in fact almost certainly dative (purpose): the dative in -u, while uncommon, is not incorrect.

" 'En,' inquam, 'paratum tibi adest ientaculum.' Et cum
dicto manticam meam humero exuo, caseum cum pane
propere ei porrigo, et, 'Iuxta platanum istam residamus,' aio.
[19]   "Quo facto et ipse aliquid indidem sumo, eumque
avide essitantem aspiciens, aliquanto intentiore macie atque
pallore buxeo deficientem video. Sic denique eum vitalis color
turbaverat ut mihi prae metu, nocturnas etiam Furias illas
imaginanti, frustulum panis quod primum sumpseram,
quamvis admodum modicum, mediis faucibus inhaereret ac
neque deorsum demeare neque sursum remeare posset. Nam
et crebritas ipsa commeantium metum mihi cumulabat. Quis

350

355

---

349. et cum dicto: see note above, 1.6 (line 103).

350. humero: ablative of separation, "from my shoulder" (*humero < humerus = umerus*).

[19]

353. essitantem: present participle (< *essitare*) with *eum* (accusative), direct object of *video*.

354. deficientem: also with *eum*.

buxeo < *buxeus:* "yellowish." *pallor* itself literally means "green-ness," so the adjective is consistent with the result of a paling green.

vitalis color: lit., "life-sustaining color" (i.e., complexion). *vitalis* here is probably used euphemistically; editors suggest, and translators render, "deadly."

sic...eum...color turbaverat ut mihi...frustulum...inhaereret: a long result clause: "his color...altered him so much that for me...the scrap...stuck."

355. mihi, prae metu...Furias... imaginanti: "for me, conjuring images of the Furies out of fear." The Furies were the snake-haired goddesses of vengeance who pursued and drove mad those who committed capital crimes.

359. crebritas: "density," is an emendation (*<cre>br[ev]itas*) of the MSS *brevitas*, "scarcity," an unusual sense for that word with which editors are uncomfortable. Helm first suggested *paucitas*, thus supplying a better word for the meaning that seems required here, but in his third edition returned to *brevitas*; Apuleius is fond of using words in unusual or strained senses; both Scobie and Molt support the choice of *brevitas*.

commeantium: genitive pl., present participle (< *commeare*), "of those going with (us)."

quis...crederet: deliberative question, "Who...would believe?"

360   enim de duobus comitum alterum sine alterius noxa
peremptum crederet? Verum ille, ut satis detruncaverat
cibum, sitire impatienter coeperat. Nam et optimi casei
bonam partem avide devoraverat, et haud ita longe radices
platani lenis fluvius in speciem placidae paludis ignavus ibat,
365   argento vel vitro aemulus in colorem. 'En,' inquam, 'explere
latice fontis lacteo.' Adsurgit ille et, oppertus paululum
planiorem ripae marginem, complicitus in genua appronat
se avidus affectans poculum. Necdum satis extremis labiis

360. de duobus comitum alterum: "(that) the second of two companions."

alterum...peremptum (esse): indirect statement, "that the second...had been done in."

361. ut...detruncaverat: "when... he had devoured." The use of the temporal conjunction (*ut* or *cum*) with the imperfect or pluperfect indicative, in theory, defines only the time of the main verb, not the attendant circumstances, for which the subjunctive is usual. It would be the equivalent, then, of *postquam*. In practice, the connection between the temporal clause and the main clause often involves more than mere time, as here. For the meaning of the verb, see note on *contruncare* in 1.4 (line 54), above. The violence of the word in this passage reflects the manner of Socrates' literally "attacking" his food.

362. coeperat...devoraverat: pluperfects used for perfects; see note on *ieceras* in 1.3 (line 46), above.

363. haud ita longe: "not so far (from)," used here virtually as a preposition (+ accusative) with *radices platani.*

This is an odd construction, apparently on analogy with *prope*. In his third edition, Helm suggested that *ibat* should be emended to *praeteribat*, so that the prefix *praeter-* would govern the accusative *radices*.

364. in speciem: "looking like."

365. explere: 2nd person singular, present passive imperative, lit., "be filled," or "fill yourself up."

366. latice...lacteo: "with the milky liquid," a vivid, but perhaps a bit unsettling, image.

oppertus (< *opperior*): "having waited (for)."

367. appronat se: "he laid himself face down."

368. poculum: "a drink." This is an example of metonymy ("cup" used to mean "drink").

necdum satis: "not yet quite." The clauses *necdum...et* (where *et* functions like *cum*) provide a kind of inverted *cum*-clause: rather than "When X happened, Y..." the idea is expressed as "X had [not] happened...and (=when)."

summum aquae rorem attigerat, et iugulo eius vulnus dehiscit

370   in profundum patorem et illa spongia de eo repente devolvitur

eamque parvus admodum comitatur cruor. Denique corpus

exanimatum in flumen paene cernuat, nisi ego altero eius

pede retento vix et aegre ad ripam superiorem adtraxi, ubi

defletum pro tempore comitem misellum arenosa humo in

375   amnis vicinia sempiterna contexi. Ipse trepidus et eximie

metuens mihi per diversas et avias solitudines aufugi, et quasi

conscius mihi caedis humanae relicta patria et Lare ultroneum

---

369. iugulo: ablative of location, "at his throat."

vulnus dehiscit: the curse invoked above at 1.13 is now fulfilled.

370. in profundum patorem: "into a deep opening."

372. cernuat (< *cernuo, cernuāre*, from *cernuus, -a, -um*): "falls head first." The present is used for narrative vividness. The condition (*nisi*) is past unreal (contrary to fact), but Apuleius uses the indicative in both clauses. The use of the present tense is highly colored. This manner of speech is becoming increasingly common in American English: "If he runs faster, he gets there on time," meaning "If he **had** run ..., he **would have** gotten there ..."

373. pede retento could be taken as an ablative absolute, but it could also be understood simply as an ablative of means (*pede*) described by an adjective that happens to be a participle.

adtraxi: supply a direct object such as *eum* or *illum*. The perfect indicative is used instead of the pluperfect subjunctive. See note above on *cernuat*.

374. defletum...comitem... contexi: "I covered my wept-over friend," or "I wept over my friend and covered him." This action also fulfills the terms of Meroë's curse in 1.13.

375. amnis ("stream") is genitive; the noun with *in* is *viciniā*.

sempiterna: neuter pl. used as an adverb.

376. quasi conscius mihi caedis humanae: "as if feeling guilty for the murder of a human being."

377. relictā patriā et Lare: ablative absolute, "after abandoning my country and my home." The use of *Lar* ("household god") for *domus* is an example of metonymy.

ultroneum exilium: "voluntary exile."

exilium amplexus, nunc Aetoliam novo contracto matrimonio colo."

380   **[20]**   Haec Aristomenes. At ille comes eius, qui statim initio obstinata incredulitate sermonem eius respuebat, "Nihil," inquit, "hac fabula fabulosius, nihil isto mendacio absurdius." Et ad me conversus, "Tu autem," inquit, "vir ut habitus et habitudo demonstrat ornatus, accedis huic fabulae?"

385   "Ego vero," inquam, "nihil impossibile arbitror, sed utcumque fata decreverint, ita cuncta mortalibus provenire. Nam et mihi et tibi et cunctis hominibus multa usu venire

---

378. Aetoliam...colo: "I live in Aetolia."

novo contracto matrimonio: ablative absolute, "after acquiring a new marriage," or "and I have re-married."

[20]

Arrival in Hypata (20–21). So ends the tale of Aristomenes. Lucius comments that he is fully prepared to believe the story, and furthermore is grateful for its entertainment value, which distracted him from the tedium of the journey. At the same moment, the travelers arrive at their destination of Hypata, and Aristomenes and his companion set off to pursue their own affairs. Lucius asks for directions to the house of one Milo, where he hopes for lodging.

381. obstinata incredulitate: Aristomenes' companion is re-introduced as the skeptical foil to Lucius' open-mindedness.

nihil...fabulosius: "nothing... more fictional," **...nihil...absurdius:** "nothing... more ridiculous."

382. hāc fabulā...isto mendacio: ablatives of comparison, "**than** this story,"..."**than** that lie."

383. vir...ornatus: "a refined gentleman."

386. decreverint: perfect subjunctive, a primary tense of the subjunctive: subordinate clauses in indirect statement (see next note) are in the subjunctive.

provenire: "happens," infinitive in indirect statement, depending on *arbitror*.

387. multa...mira et paene infecta: "many wondrous and almost impossible things."

usu venire: "come from experience."

390

mira et paene infecta, quae tamen ignaro relata fidem perdant.
Sed ego huic et credo hercules et gratas gratias memini, quod
lepidae fabulae festivitate nos avocavit, asperam denique ac
prolixam viam sine labore ac taedio evasi. Quod beneficium
etiam illum vectorem meum credo laetari, sine fatigatione
sui me usque ad istam civitatis portam non dorso illius sed
meis auribus provecto."

388. infecta: "impossible," i.e., "not able to be done, never done before" rather than "not done," just as in the use of *invictus* to mean "unconquerable."

quae ignaro relata: "which, when reported to one who is ignorant of them."

389. sed ego ...: Lucius expresses his willingness to believe in marvels of all kinds.

gratas gratias: Apuleius is fond of such jingles (see above, 1.7 [line 131], *gratae atque gratuitae*). The accusative with *memini* is as regular as the genitive.

memini: "I am storing up in memory."

390. lepidae fabulae: the charming nature of the story would redeem it

whether or not it is true. In the Prologue, the narrator listed pleasure and entertainment as chief virtues in story-telling.

391. quod beneficium = *Et hoc beneficium* (nominative), linking *Qui.*

392. illum vectorem: "that bearer," i.e., *illum equum*. In 1.15 (line 285), above, Apuleius used *convector* in this sense.

sine fatigatione sui: lit., "without weariness of itself," or "without causing any weariness to itself." *sui* here is a good example of the use of the genitive case of the pronoun: it is not possessive (which would have been the adjective *suā*), but an objective genitive (*fatigatio* **for** whom, not belonging to whom).

393. me...provecto: ablative absolute, "since I...was carried."

395   **[21]**   Is finis nobis et sermonis et itineris communis fuit. Nam comites uterque ad villulam proximam laevorsum abierunt. Ego vero quod primum ingressui stabulum conspicatus sum accessi, et de quadam anu caupona ilico percontor. "Estne," inquam, "Hypata haec civitas?" Adnuit.

400   "Nostine Milonem quendam e primoribus?" Arrisit, et "Vere," inquit, "primus istic perhibetur Milo, qui extra pomerium et urbem totam colit."

    "Remoto," inquam, "ioco, parens optima, dic oro et cuiatis sit et quibus deversetur aedibus."

[21]

396. comites uterque: "my companions each," rather than "both (pl.) my companions."

laevorsum: "off to the left." Thus Lucius arrives at his destination alone, and it is clear that Apuleius' only narrative purposes for including the travelers in the story were to present the tale and to highlight the issue of credence in marvels or second-hand reports.

397. quod primum...stabulum conspicatus sum: this is normal Latin word order, where the antecedent of the relative pronoun (here *stabulum*) has been attracted into the relative clause itself; logically, the order should have been: *primum stabulum quod conspicatus sum.*

398. de quadam anu: "from an old woman." The use of *de* instead of *ab* with the verb of asking is a colloquialism.

cauponā = *copā,* a female innkeeper (in apposition to *anu*).

400. Nostine = *No(vi)sti-ne:* "do you know?"

e primoribus: "(one) of the leading citizens." The old woman picks up on the implied comparative in *primores* and puns on *primus:* the joke in this sentence is that Milo is naturally **first**, since you get to him before you even get to the city.

401. perhibetur: "is held (to be)," one of a number of Latin words that can mean "is regarded" (like *habetur, ducitur*). *Perhibetur* is an emphatic form of *habetur.*

extra pomerium et urbem totam is all part of the same prepositional phrase (i.e., *urbem* is not the direct object of *colit,* which is used synonymously with *habitat*).

403. remoto...ioco: ablative absolute, "joking aside."

cuiatis: "where he is from, what nationality he is." See note on *cuiatis* in 1.5 (line 77), above.

404. quibus...aedibus: ablative of location.

deversetur < *deversor:* "be put up, dwell, live."

405   "Videsne," inquit, "extremas fenestras, quae foris urbem prospiciunt, et altrinsecus fores proximum respicientes angiportum? Inibi iste Milo deversatur, ampliter nummatus et longe opulentus, verum extremae avaritiae et sordis infimae infamis homo. Faenus denique copiosum sub arrabone auri

410   et argenti crebriter exercens, exiguo Lare inclusus et aerugini semper intentus, cum uxorem etiam calamitatis suae comitem habeat, neque praeter unicam pascit ancillulam, et habitu mendicantis semper incedit."

---

405. forīs: the adverb, "out(side)" (used as a play against *fores* in the next line).

406. fores...respicientes: "door-posts...looking back" (direct object of *vides*).

407. angiportum: "alley-way," defined by ancient writers as a narrow and twisty street where carts cannot be driven.

ampliter is a word from Roman comedy, presumably colloquial.

409. infamis homo: "a man with a bad reputation (for, + genitive)." *infamis* is a strongly pejorative word. Note the jingle on *infimae* and *infamis*.

faenus...crebriter exercens: "(although) constantly practicing money-lending." *faenus* (neuter) is the direct object of *exercens*, nominative.

sub arrabone: "with security (on the loan), with collateral." *arrabo* is considered colloquial (the technical term at

law was *arra*). Note the assonance of *sub arrabone et auri et argenti*.

410. exiguo Lare: "(in) a small house" (lit., a small household **god**). Apuleius seems fond of this metonymy.

411. cum uxorem...habeat: *cum* is concessive, "although;" *comitem* is in apposition to *uxorem*; *calamitatis suae*, "of **his** disaster" (*suae* referring to Milo, not the wife, and agreeing with *calamitatis*). The MSS read *cum uxore...comite habeat*, which some editors prefer, changing *habeat* to *habet*, understanding *cum* as the preposition, and *habet* = *habitat*: "he lives with his wife...as," rather than "although he has a wife...as."

412. praeter unicam...ancillulam: "a maidservant, except for one only."

pascit: "keeps, maintains," the normal word for supporting slaves, also used for the upkeep of soldiers. See *Oxford Latin Dictionary*, s.v. *pasco* 1d and 3a.

Ad haec ego risum subicio. "Benigne," inquam, "et

415   prospicue Demeas meus in me consuluit, qui peregrinaturum

tali viro conciliavit, in cuius hospitio nec fumi nec nidoris

nebulam vererer."

[22]   Et cum dicto modico secus progressus ostium accedo

et ianuam firmiter oppessulatam pulsare vocaliter incipio.

420   Tandem adulescentula quaedam procedens, "Heus tu,"

inquit, "qui tam fortiter fores verberasti, sub qua specie

---

415. prospicue: "with foresight, thoughtfully."

in me consuluit: "advised me." *consulere* with *in* + accusative usually means "ask" advice, as opposed to "give" advice (which is usually *consulere* + dative).

(me) peregrinaturum: direct object, "me as I was about to set out."

416. (me)...conciliavit: "recommended me...to, assured the good graces of...for me."

in cuius hospitio...vererer: relative clause of characteristic (subjunctive), "(that sort of man) in whose house...I need fear." Lucius jokes that he is just as glad that Milo is frugal, because he doesn't have to put up with the fumes of good cooking.

[22]

At the house of Milo (22–26). The Book concludes after Lucius arrives in Hypata and seeks out a man named Milo, for whom he has a letter of introduction. Lucius was traveling on business (1.2, above), but we are not told what this business is. Milo accepts Lucius as a guest, but treats him rather shabbily.

Arrival and introductions (22–23). After some delay, Lucius is admitted to Milo's house, and gives him a letter from one Demeas, a mutual acquaintance. Milo is aware of Lucius' connections with the local aristocracy, and invites him to share his (meager) dinner and a modest room, as well as to have a bath.

418. et cum dicto: see note on 1.6 (line 103), above.

419. oppessulatam: "bolted."

pulsare vocaliter incipio: "I started to bang in a loud voice," a mixed metaphor.

421. verberasti = *verbera(vi)sti.*

sub qua specie: "under what category?" since, as she goes on to say, he has no gold or silver with him. *species* has the sense, in business language, of "subdivision," "species," "specific form," or "visible character."

mutuari cupis? An tu solus ignoras praeter aurum argentumque nullum nos pignus admittere?"

"Meliora," inquam, "ominare, et potius responde an intra

425 aedes erum tuum offenderim."

"Plane," inquit, "sed quae causa quaestionis huius?"

"Litteras ei a Corinthio Demea scriptas ad eum reddo."

"Dum annuntio," inquit, "hic ibidem me opperimino."

Et cum dicto rursum foribus oppessulatis intro capessivit.

430 Modico deinde regressa patefactis foribus, "Rogat te," inquit.

Intuli me eumque accubantem exiguo admodum grabatulo et commodum cenare incipientem invenio. Adsidebat pedes

---

422. mutuari: "to be given a loan." The Latin noun for loan is *mutuum*. She assumes that the only reason anyone would visit Milo would be to get some money.

423. nullum...pignus: "no...collateral." A *pignus* was a deposit or an object given as security against the loan.

424. meliora...ominare: "Give better omens." *ominare* is imperative (< *ominor*).

425. offenderim: "I may find." Perfect subjunctive in an indirect question (introduced by *an*).

427. a Corinthio Demea: "from Demeas of Corinth."

428. opperimino: the ending *-mino* is future passive (deponent) imperative, rare and archaic.

429. et cum dicto: see note on 1.6 (line 103).

(se) capessivit: lit., "she took herself," or "she went."

431. intuli me: "I took myself in," or "I entered."

eum accubantem...et cenare incipientem invenio: "I found him reclining...and beginning to eat."

432. adsidebat pedes uxor: "his wife was seated at his feet." It was an old-fashioned custom that women did not recline in company, but rather (if present at all) sat. At Rome, this custom began to change around the time of Augustus. But the verb here may be used vaguely, because a little below Milo urges Lucius to take his wife's spot and apologizes for (or explains) the lack of places to sit (*sessibula*). This picture may also explain why Milo asks his wife to withdraw. Scobie and Molt, on the other hand, infer that Milo was holding his wife to old-fashioned customs, that their relationship was rather formal and distant, and that it was unusual for the wife to withdraw during business discussions.

uxor et mensa vacua posita, cuius monstratu, "En," inquit, "hospitium."

435 "Bene," ego, et ilico ei litteras Demeae trado. Quibus properiter lectis, "Amo," inquit, "meum Demean, qui mihi tantum conciliavit hospitem."

[23] Et cum dicto iubet uxorem decedere, utque in eius locum adsidam iubet, meque etiam nunc verecundia

440 cunctantem adrepta lacinia detrahens, "Adside," inquit, "istic.

433. mensā vacuā positā: ablative absolute, "an empty table having been laid" or "(sitting) near an empty table."

cuius monstratu: "with a gesture at which."

en...hospitium: "here is our fare" (for guests).

436. properiter seems to be colloquial for *propere*.

amo meum Demean: "I thank my friend Demeas," a fairly common conversational use of *amare*.

437. tantum...hospitem: "such a distinguished guest."

conciliavit: see note on section 1.21 (line 416), above.

[23]

438. et cum dicto: see note on 1.6 (line 103).

in eius locum: "in **her** place."

ut...adsidam iubet: "he asked me to be seated." In Classical Latin, the construction with *iubere* was accusative + infinitive; the indirect command (*ut* + subjunctive) can also be found in early Latin.

439. me...cunctantem...detrahens: "(he ...) dragging me down as I was hesitating."

verecundiā: "from shyness, modesty." Scobie (124) notes that *verecundia* is a consistent attribute of Lucius, even when he has been changed into a beast. Here his *verecundia* may have resulted from being asked to take the place on Milo's couch where his wife had just been reclining (but see note above, 1.22 [line 432], on *adsidebat*).

440. adreptā laciniā: ablative absolute, "grabbing me by the border (of my tunic)," perhaps an example of synecdoche, the naming of a part of something in place of the whole thing.

Nam prae metu latronum nulla sessibula ac ne sufficientem
supellectilem parare nobis licet." Feci.

Et sic, "Ego te," inquit, "etiam de ista corporis speciosa
habitudine deque hac virginali prorsus verecundia, generosa

445   stirpe proditum et recte conicerem, sed et meus Demeas eadem
litteris pronuntiat. Ergo brevitatem gurgustioli nostri ne
spernas peto. Erit tibi adiacens [et] ecce illud cubiculum
honestum receptaculum. Fac libenter deverseris in nostro.
Nam et maiorem domum dignatione tua feceris, et tibi specimen

441. prae metu latronum: "for fear of robbers." *Prae* is used with the ablative to be "in view of, because of;" with the accusative it usually means "ahead of, in front of."

ne: "not...(even)": the usual ... *quidem* is omitted.

443. ego te...generosa stirpe proditum (esse)...conicerem: "I would guess that you were endowed with noble breeding." *conicerem* is imperfect subjunctive in the apodosis of a present unreal (contrary to fact) condition; the protasis is not stated.

de...speciosa habitudine deque hac virginali...verecundia: "on the basis of... atttractive appearance and of this maidenly modesty."

445. eadem: accusative pl. n., direct object, "this same judgment."

446. brevitatem = *parvitatem.*

gurgustioli: genitive s., "little hovel." A *gurgustium* was a poor hovel; the diminutive (*-olum*) need not imply smallness, but rather attaches an emotional flavor to the word from Milo's point of view.

ne spernas peto: "please do not shrink (from)." *ne spernas* is an indirect command depending on *peto.*

447. erit tibi: dative of possession, "you shall have."

[et] ecce: the *et* seems intrusive, and editors usually either delete it as a copyist's error from *ecce,* or emend to *en* (Haupt's suggestion), which would provide a typically Apuleian redundancy. In his third edition, Helm has accepted *et* (no brackets).

448. honestum receptaculum: in apposition to *cubiculum.* On the diminutive (< *receptus,* "refuge, retreat"), see note above on *gurgustioli.* Here the repetition of the sound (*cubiculum...receptaculum*) may have influenced the usage.

fac deverseris: "be sure to stay" (*deverseris < deversor*).

449. et...feceris, et...adrogaris: "you will **both** have made..., **and** taken up." *adrogaris = adroga(ve)ris.*

dignatione tua: "by your rank, reputation."

tibi specimen gloriosum: "a shining example for yourself."

450   gloriosum adrogaris, si contentus Lare parvulo Thesei illius
       cognominis patris tui virtutes aemulaveris, qui non est
       aspernatus Hecales anus hospitium tenue."

           Et vocata ancillula, "Fotis," inquit, "sarcinulas hospitis
       susceptas cum fide conde in illud cubiculum, ac simul ex
455   promptuario oleum unctui et lintea tersui et cetera hoc eidem

---

450. Lare parvulo = *domo parvula*, the same metonymy as in 1.8 (line 145), 1.19 (line 377), and 1.21 (line 410), above.

Thesei illius...virtutes: "the virtues of that famous Theseus." The position of the demonstrative *illius* is emphatic.

451. cognominis patris tui: hence we discover that Lucius' father was named Theseus. It is not clear whether the word *cognomen* is to be taken as meaning that he had a *praenomen* and *nomen* in the Roman fashion, or whether *cognomen* is used loosely. If the former, his name would be a hybrid of Roman and Greek, a pattern characteristic of freedmen. It is by no means certain that the Lucius of our story should be taken to be Apuleius himself; hence, no biographical conclusions should be drawn about the author.

452. Hecalēs: a Greek first declension genitive singular, in apposition to *anūs*. There was a district (deme) in Attica named Hecale; in legend, an old woman with that name had entertained the hero Theseus on his way to fight the Bull of Marathon, but she died before he returned. Theseus founded a cult in her honor to Zeus Hekaleios. The poet Callimachus wrote a narrative poem about her. Milo establishes the association between Lucius' father Theseus and the legendary Theseus in order to make a modest comment about his own wealth. In reality, Milo was simply stingy with his wealth, while Hecale was poor but generous.

453. Fotis: the spelling of the name varies in the MSS between "Photis" and "Fotis." I have regularized each occurrence for the sake of consistency. The Greek name Photis would connote "light" (from φῶς [phōs]), the source of the English word "photon," also found (for example) in "photography."

sarcinulas...conde: "store the bags."

454. ex promptuario: "from the store-room" (< *promptuarium*).

455. oleum unctui: "oil for rubbing." *unctui*, dative < *unctus, -ūs, m.* <*unguēre*, "to rub."

tersui: "for wiping," dative < *tersus, -ūs, m.* < *tergēre*, "to wipe off."

hoc = *huc*.

eidem usui: double dative, "for his use."

usui profer ociter, et hospitem meum produc ad proximas balneas; satis arduo itinere atque prolixo fatigatus est."

[24]   His ego auditis, mores atque parsimoniam ratiocinans Milonis volensque me artius ei conciliare, "Nihil," inquam,

460   "rerum istarum, quae itineris ubique nos comitantur, indigemus. Sed et balneas facile percontabimur. Plane quod est mihi summe praecipuum, equo, qui me strenue pervexit, faenum atque hordeum acceptis istis nummulis tu, Fotis, emito."

---

456. ociter: "quickly," does not appear before Apuleius. The comparative form *ocius* is common, and was used instead of the positive form in other preserved texts.

457. satis: "quite," i.e, an **intensive** adverb (as often) rather than "sufficiently."

---

[24]

Side-trip to the market (24–25). Hoping to impress his host with his own good will, and unimpressed by the fare he was being offered, Lucius goes off to the forum to buy his own dinner. He bargains for some fish, whereupon he encounters an old schoolmate named Pythias, who is a local magistrate. Pythias feels that Lucius has been cheated and takes him back to the forum, where he abuses the fish-monger who sold Lucius the fish.

458. ratiocinans: "reflecting upon."

459. artius: comparative adverb, "more closely" (< *artus*).

460. itineris ubique: "on every part of my journey."

461. percontabimur: "I will find out (about)."

The word order of this sentence is remarkably choppy, and suggests that Lucius was stumbling a bit for the right words. Natural word order would have been: *tu, Fotis, acceptis his nummulis, emito faenum atque hordeum equo, qui...* Lucius hopes that his offer to supply his own bath gear and pay for his horse's feed will get him into Milo's good graces.

quod est mihi summe praecipuum: "what is most important to me."

462. equo,...faenum atque hordeum: "hay and barley for my horse" (*equo* is dative).

464. emito: future imperative < *emere*.

465   His actis et rebus meis in illo cubiculo conditis, pergens

ipse ad balneas, ut prius aliquid nobis cibatui prospicerem,

forum cupidinis peto inque eo piscatum opiparem exposi-

tum video, et percontato pretio, quod centum nummis

indicaret, aspernatus viginti denariis praestinavi. Inde me

470   commodum egredientem continatur Pythias condiscipulus

466. cibatui: "for eating," dative < *cibatus* < *cibus*.

467. forum cupidinis: a playful twist on the usual spelling, *forum cuppedinis*, "the morsel market" (*cuppedinis* < *cuppedo*, "dainty, treat"). Apuleius' use of *cupido* rather than *cuppedo* invokes the sense, "desire." According to Festus (48L), delicacies were called *cuppes* or *cuppedia*, hence the name of the market. Although the scene of the tale is set in Hypata, there is a strong Roman coloring to the action; in Rome itself, the *forum cuppedinis* was near (or the same as) the Macellum, on the Via Sacra (Varro, *LL* 5.146). Editors used to emend *cupidinis* to *cuppedinis* as a copyist's error, but it is now standard to attribute the word-play to Apuleius. (Still another play is possible, if there was in fact a Forum Cupidinis ["market of Cupid/Eros"] in Hypata.)

piscatum opiparem expositum: "a sumptuous catch of fish on display." The form *opiparem* is third declension; the Classical form of the adjective is *opiparum* (1st-2nd declension).

468. quod centum nummis indi- caret: "which he wanted to set at 100 coins (sesterces)." *indicaret* is subjunctive, either potential or characteristic.

469. aspernatus: "I rejected (this and...)."

viginti denariis: "for 20 denarii." 100 sesterces was equivalent to 25 de- narii, so Lucius had negotiated a 20% price reduction. Summers (1971) notes that the language of the transaction is appropriate to a formal contract of sale at Roman Law.

470. continatur < *continor, contin- ari, continatus sum*: "encounter" — this word occurs in Sisenna (a historian) and Apuleius, another example of either ar- chaism or use of a word that has faded from literary use but remained in com- mon parlance.

Pythias condiscipulus: "Pythias, my fellow student." More biographical details about our main character emerge. The name Pythias was an epithet of Apollo and gives the title ("Pythia") to his priestess at Delphi; it comes from the Greek verb πυνθάνω [pynthanō], which means "find out upon inquiry." Perhaps Pythias' name characterizes him as an "interrogator."

apud Athenas: an unusual sub- stitution for the locative (*Athenis*), "in Athens."

apud Athenas Atticas meus, qui me post aliquantum multum
temporis amanter agnitum invadit, amplexusque ac comiter
deosculatus, "Mi Luci," ait, "sat pol diu est quod intervisimus
te, at hercules exinde cum a Clytio magistro digressi sumus.
475   Quae autem tibi causa peregrinationis huius?"

**471. qui me...amanter agnitum in-
vadit:** "who...lovingly rushed upon me (as
I was) recognized." Some editors propose
transposing the word order of *amanter*
and *agnitum* to facilitate understanding
amanter with *invadit*. On the other hand,
it is possible that *amanter* actually colors
both *agnitum* and *invadit*.

post aliquantum multum temporis:
"after so long a time." Editors suspect that
aliquantum is a misspelling for (or mis-
copying of) *aliquam* (adverb); Apuleius
uses the combination *aliquam multum* in
two other passages of the *Metamorphoses*
(5.26, 11.26). *temporis* is genitive of the
whole, which is commonly used with
expressions of indefinite quantity, such
as *satis, plus, nimis,* and the like.

473. mi Luci: vocative: the vocative
of *meus* is irregular, and that of Lucius is
the regular contraction of nouns that end
in -*ius* (*filius* > *fili*).

sat...diu est: "It's been quite a long
time." *sat* (= *satis*) is intensive, as in 1.23
(line 457), above.

pol: a mild oath, "by Pollux" (see
note above on 1.8 [line 139]).

quod: "since." The use of *quod* as a
temporal word is archaic.

474. hercules = *mehercule*, another
mild oath, "by Hercules."

exinde: "from the time."

"Crastino die scies," inquam. "Sed quid istud? Voti gaudeo. Nam et lixas et virgas et habitum prorsus magistratui congruentem in te video."

"Annonam curamus," ait, "et aedilem gerimus, et si quid
480   obsonare cupis utique commodabimus." Abnuebam, quippe

476. quid istud? Lucius reacts to Pythias' dress, and the apparatus of his office.

voti gaudeo: "I rejoice at the (fulfillment of your) prayer" or "I rejoice at the prayer (I must offer)." *gaudere* can be followed by genitive (as here) or ablative to show the cause of the joy. A *votum* could be either a prayer offered in acknowledgment of someone else's fortune, or one given to secure one's own fortune ("vow"). In either case, the expression means, "I congratulate you." Here Lucius makes a little joke, implying that Pythias had prayed for an important political office.

477. lixas: "attendants" (< *lixa, -ae*, f.) Lucius, being a Greek speaker, seems to use the wrong word (only Apuleius uses the word in this sense) instead of the correct Latin *lictores* ("magistrate's attendants"); in standard Latin, *lixa* means "camp follower." Pythias claims to be an Aedile, but they are not entitled to *lictores* and they are not found as such outside Rome. Roman Aediles did not have *imperium*, and only magistrates with *imperium* were entitled to *lictores*. (But see below, Apuleius is consistent in this portrayal.)

habitum...congruentem: "the garb that is consistent with."

479. annonam curamus: "I am in charge of the grain-supply."

aedilem gerimus: "I am serving as Aedile." Of course, the situation is Thessaly, not Rome, so it is most unlikely that Pythias should be viewed as a real Roman magistrate. If his office is to be taken seriously, and not just as a fictional device, he will have been an equivalent magistrate of the town Hypata, but the use of *lictores* in that case is problematic. In Rome, charge of the grain-supply was often awarded to a promagistrate with *imperium*, who would thus be entitled to *lictores*. The Aediles were responsible for the supervision of the markets, hence Pythias' next comment.

480. obsonare: "to shop." This word is a Greek borrowing (< ὄψ-ωνεῖν [opsōnein]), lit., "to buy fish." The word is used here precisely, whether by chance or by design.

abnuebam: "I kept refusing."

quippe qui: "because I ..." (*quippe qui* is used to show the causal connection to *abnuebam*).

qui iam cenae affatim piscatum prospexeramus. Sed enim Pythias, visa sportula succussisque in aspectum planiorem piscibus, "At has quisquilias quanti parasti?"

"Vix," inquam, "piscatori extorsimus accipere viginti

485   denarium."

[25]   Quo audito, statim adrepta dextera postliminio me in forum cupidinis reducens, "Et a quo," inquit, "istorum nugamenta haec comparasti?" Demonstro seniculum — in angulo sedebat — quem confestim pro aedilitatis imperio voce

490   asperrima increpans, "Iam iam," inquit, "nec amicis quidem

---

481. cenae: (dative), "for dinner."

482. visa sportula succussisque...piscibus: ablative absolutes, "taking a look at the basket and shaking up the fish."

483. quanti parasti: "how much did you pay for" (*parasti = para(vi)sti*). *quanti* is genitive of value.

485. denarium = *denariorum. viginti* is accusative (direct object), while *denarium* is genitive of the whole, "twenty of (my) denarii." Perhaps we are to envision Lucius holding out his purse with some coins still in it.

[25]

486. postliminio: adverbial, "back." The use of this word with this meaning is a mannerism of Apuleius, occurring six other times in this work. In this particular passage, he may be invoking its technical sense, "by right of civil return," as a pompous hyperbole consistent with the character of Pythias. *Postiliminium* technically was the right at Roman Law for citizens captured in war to return to their original civil status if they escaped or were freed.

488. nugamenta haec = *has nugas.*

seniculum (= *senem*): the use of the diminutive emphasizes the pathetic

character of the old man in the face of a Roman magistrate accompanied by lictors.

489. quem...increpans: "and (Pythias, while) scolding him." The change of subject is abrupt.

pro aedilitatis imperio: "in proportion to the power of an aedile." Roman Aediles, strictly speaking, did not possess *imperium*, but Lucius sustains a consistent story.

490. nec...vel omnino: "neither...or at all," a somewhat awkward pairing.

nostris vel omnino ullis hospitibus parcitis, quod tam magnis
pretiis pisces frivolos indicatis et florem Thessalicae regionis
ad instar solitudinis et scopuli edulium caritate deducitis?
Sed non impune. Iam enim faxo scias quemadmodum sub

495   meo magisterio mali debeant coerceri." Et profusa in medium
sportula iubet officialem suum insuper pisces inscendere ac
pedibus suis totos obterere.

    Qua contentus morum severitudine meus Pythias ac mihi
ut abirem suadens, "Sufficit mihi, o Luci," inquit, "seniculi

500   tanta haec contumelia."

---

491. parcitis...indicatis...deducitis: it is not clear why Pythias addresses the old man in the plural, for he is clearly berating only one man. Evidently, he is generalizing about the fishmongers in general while yelling specifically at one old man.

tam magnis pretiis: ablative of price.

493. ad instar solitudinis et scopuli: "to the likeness of a wilderness and a cliff." This is probably an example of hendiadys, where "wilderness and a cliff" means "a wilderness cliff."

edulium: "of (your) foodstuffs" (genitive < *edulia* < *edo, edere*).

caritate: "by the costliness" (lit., "**dear**ness," the same metaphor as in English).

494. faxo scias: "I shall make sure that you know." *scias* is a subjunctive in a result clause (common after forms of *facere*); *faxo* is an archaic future perfect (used here by Pythias to sound official).

495. coerceri: "to be compelled". A magistrate with *imperium* had the right of *coercitio*, which was basically the right to order citizens around. The dramatic powers of Pythias remain consistent.

496. officialem: "attendant."

497. totos obterere: "to grind them all down" (*totos* = *omnes*, a colloquialism).

498. qua contentus... severitudine: "and satisfied with this harshness." *qua* = *et hāc* (linking *Qui*) and agrees with *severitudine* (ablative).

morum: genitive pl. < *mos*, "of character."

499. ut abirem suadens: "urging me to leave." *ut abirem* is an indirect command. Apuleius uses secondary sequence, even though the main verb (*inquit*) is present tense, because he is thinking of the whole passage as a narrative of past events.

seniculi...contumelia: "abuse of the old man." Thus Pythias makes a gratuitous display of his authority and Lucius ends up with no dinner after all.

His actis consternatus ac prorsus obstupidus, ad balneas me refero, prudentis condiscipuli valido consilio et nummis simul privatus et cena, lautusque ad hospitium Milonis ac dehinc cubiculum me reporto.

505   [26]   Et ecce Fotis ancilla, "Rogat te," inquit, "hospes." At ego iam inde Milonis abstinentiae cognitor excusavi comiter, quod viae vexationem non cibo sed somno censerem diluendam. Isto accepto pergit ipse et iniecta dextera clementer me trahere adoritur. Ac dum cunctor, dum modeste
510   renitor, "Non prius," inquit, "discedam quam me sequaris."

---

502. prudentis: "wise," ironic.

valido consilio: "because of the energetic help," ironic.

et **nummis...***et* **cena:** "both of my money and of my dinner." *nummis* and *cenā* are ablatives of separation, the usual construction with *privare*.

503. lautus-que: "and having bathed" (< *lavare*).

504. dehinc: "after that."

me reporto = *me refero* (a colloquialism).

[26]

A long evening with Milo (26). Lucius returns to Milo's house unfed and unrefreshed, hoping only to go to bed and rest from his journey, but Milo insists that he stay up and talk, answering endless inquiries about his friend Demeas and his affairs until late in the night.

506. Milonis abstinentiae cognitor: "a man fully aware of Milo's stinginess."

507. quod...censerem: "because (I said)...I thought." The subjunctive with

quod indicates an "alleged" cause; the indicative presents the cause as a fact.

viae vexationem...diluendam (esse): "(that) the discomfort of my journey should be washed away."

508. isto accepto: ablative absolute, "upon hearing this."

509. adoritur: "he tried." The word is not uncommon in this sense, but it has a forceful connotation appropriate to Milo's insistence.

Et dictum iure iurando secutus iam obstinationi suae me
ingratis oboedientem perducit ad illum suum grabatulum, et
residenti "Quam salve agit," inquit, "Demeas noster? Quid
uxor? Quid liberi? Quid vernaculi?"

515   Narro singula. Percontatur accuratius causas etiam
peregrinationis meae. Quas ubi probe protuli, iam et de patria
nostra et eius primoribus ac denique de ipso praeside
scrupulosissime explorans, ubi me post itineris tam saevi
vexationem sensit fabularum quoque serie fatigatum in verba
520   media somnolentum desinere ac nequicquam, defectum iam,

---

511. et dictum iure iurando secutus: "and following up his statement (*dictum*) with an oath (*iure iurando*)."

obstinationi: dative after *oboedientem*.

me ingratis oboedientem: direct object, "me, obeying against my will."

513. residenti: dative, "(to me) as I was sitting down." Milo's continued interrogation of his tired and hungry guest is boorish behavior. Lucius maintains a polite facade throughout.

514. vernaculi: "his family slaves," diminutive of *verna*. A *verna* was a slave born in the household where she or he was now serving.

515. narro singula: "I answered each individual question," or "I told the stories one at a time."

516. quas = *Et has* (linking *Qui*).

protuli: "I explained." Most editors recommend emendation to the more usual *pertuli*; the error would have been easy, since the prefixes (*pro-* and *per-*) were routinely abbreviated in MSS with a stroke above or below a "p."

iam...concederam: This long period consists of an extended main thought of which Milo is the subject (*iam...explorans, ubi...sensit,...tandem patitur:* "now investigating,...when he noticed,...he finally allowed"), an indirect statement which depends on *sensit*, of which Lucius is the subject (*me...fatigatum...somnolentum desinere ac...defectum...balbuttire:* "that I...worn out...and sleepy was stopping and...exhausted...I was stammering"), and a result clause: *patitur cubitum concederem,* "he allowed me to go off to bed." The convoluted sentence perhaps reflects Lucius' state of mind at the time.

517. eius primoribus: "its leading citizens" (*eius* refers to *patria*).

518. post...vexationem: "after the tribulation."

519. fabularum quoque serie: "also by the succession of stories."

incerta verborum salebra balbuttire, tandem patitur cubitum concederem. Evasi aliquando rancidi senis loquax et
famelicum convivium, somno non cibo gravatus, cenatus solis
524   fabulis, et in cubiculum reversus optatae me quieti reddidi.

---

521. incerta verborum salebra: "vague pot-holes of words." *salebra* were uneven stretches of road.

522. aliquando here = *tandem*.

loquax et famelicum convivium: "talkative and famished party," personifications of *convivium*.

523. somno non cibo gravatus: contrary to his politely expressed wish to dispel his discomfort *non cibo sed somno* (above, 1.26 [line 507]).

cenatus solis fabulis: Lucius' attitude toward the restorative and nourishing power of words (above, 1.20) has been subjected to a severe test. The conclusion of the book, which displays the main character tormented by endless talk, thus inverts its beginning, which promises to prove the soothing power of words.

Bibliography

○ ◑ ◐ ● ◐ ◑ ○

Texts and Editions

The works listed here are either specific commentaries on Book 1, or general texts and commentaries consulted and referred to in the notes.

Hanson, John Arthur, *Apuleius: Metamorphoses*. The Loeb Classical Library, Cambridge, Mass.: Harvard University Press, 1989.

Helm, R., *Apulei Platonici Madaurensis Opera Quae Supersunt. Vol. I: Metamorphoseon libri XI.* Leipzig: B. G. Teubner, 1968 (1st ed. 1907, 2d ed. 1913).

Kenney, E. J., *Apuleius: Cupid & Psyche.* Cambridge Greek and Latin Classics, Cambridge University Press, 1990.

Molt, Margaretha, *Ad Apulei Madaurensis Metamorphoseon Librum Primum Commentarius Exegeticus.* Groningen: De Waal, 1938.

Purser, Louis C., *Apuleius: The Story of Cupid and Psyche.* New Rochelle, NY: Aristide D. Caratzas, Publisher, 1983 [1910].

Scobie, A., *Apuleius: Metamorphoses I. A Commentary.* Meisenheim am Glan: Verlag Anton Hain, 1975.

Translations into English

In addition to Hanson's Loeb edition (above), which has Latin and English on facing pages, the following are known to me. Of these, while each has its virtues and points of interest, Hanson, Kenney, and Walsh are readily available and are to be recommended.

Butler, H. E., *The Metamorphoses, or Golden Ass of Apuleius of Madaura*, Oxford: Clarendon Press, 1910.

Graves, R. (revised by Michael Grant), *The Transformations of Lucius, otherwise known as the Golden Ass by Lucius Apuleius*. Harmondsworth: 1990 (1950).

Kenney, E. J., *Apuleius: The Golden Ass or Metamorphoses*. New York, London: Penguin Classics, 1998.

Lindsay, J., *The Golden Ass of Apuleius*. Bloomington: Indiana University Press, 1962 (1932).

Schnur, Harry C., *The Golden Ass. Translated by William Adlington <1566>*. New York: Collier Books, 1962.

Walsh, P. G., *Apuleius: The Golden Ass*. New York: Oxford World's Classics, 1995.

Selected Works in English for Additional Reading

Abate, F. R., *Diminutives in Apuleian Latinity*. Dissertation, Ohio State University, Columbus, 1978.

Brotherton, Blanche, "The Introduction of Characters by Name in the *Metamorphoses* of Apuleius," *Classical Philolology* 29 (1934) 36–52.

Cherpack, C., "Ideas and Prose Fiction in Antiquity," *Comparative Literature Studies* 11 (1974) 185–203.

De Filippo, J., "*Curiositas* and the Platonism of Apuleius' *Golden Ass*," *American Journal of Philology* 111 (1990) 471–492.

Dowden, K., "Apuleius and the Art of Narration," *Classical Quarterly* 32 (1982) 419–435.

Drake, G. C., "Lucius' Parents, Theseus and Salvia, in the *Golden Ass*," *Papers on Language and Literature* 29 (1993) 336–345.

Edwards, M. J., "The Proem to Apuleius' *Metamorphoses*," *Hermes* 121 (1993) 375–377.

Ferguson, John, "Apuleius," *Greece and Rome* 8 (1961) 61–74.

Finkelpearl, Ellen D., *Metamorphosis of Language in Apuleius: A Study of Allusion in the Novel*. Ann Arbor: University of Michigan Press, 1998.

Frangoulides, Stavros A., "*Cui videbor veri similia dicere proferens vera?*: Aristomenes and the Witches in Apuleius' Tale of Aristomenes," *Classical Journal* 94.4 (1999) 375–91.

Ginsburg, G. N., "Rhetoric and Representation in the *Metamorphoses* of Apuleius," *Arethusa* 10 (1977) 49–61.

Haight, E. H., *Apuleius and his Influence*, New York 1963.

Harrison, S. J., "The Speaking Book: the Prologue to Apuleius' *Metamorphoses*," *Classical Quarterly* 40 (1990) 507–513.

——, "Apuleius," *Oxford Classical Dictionary* (3rd edition, S. Hornblower and A. Spawforth, eds.). Oxford: Clarendon Press, 1996, 131–132.

——, *Oxford Readings in the Roman Novel*. Oxford: the University Press, 1999.

——, *Apuleius: A Latin Sophist*. Oxford: the University Press, 2000.

Hofmann, Heinz, ed. *Latin Fiction: The Latin Novel in Context*. London and New York: Routledge, 1999.

Hijmans, B. L., and R. T. van der Paardt, (eds.), *Aspects of Apuleius'* Golden Ass, Groningen: Bouma 1978.

Ifie, J. E., and L. A. Thompson, "Rank, Social Status and Esteem in Apuleius," *Museum Africum* 6 (1977–78) 21–36.

van Kempen, A. M. M., "A Note on Apul. *Met.* I,6 (5,15)," *Mnemosyne* 33 (1980) 362–364.

Kenny, B., "The Reader's Role in The Golden Ass," *Arethusa* 7 (1974) 187–209.

Laird, A., "Fiction, Bewilderment and Story Worlds: the Implication of Claims to Truth in Apuleius," in *Lies and Fiction in the Ancient World*, C. Gill and T. P. Wiseman (eds.), Exeter, 1993, 147–174.

Mason, H. J., "The Distinction of Lucius in Apuleius' Metamorphoses," *Phoenix* 37 (1983) 135–143.

Mayrhofer, C. M., "On Two Stories in Apuleius," *Antichthon* 9 (1975) 68–80.

McCreight, Thomas D., *Rhetorical Strategies and Word Choice in Apuleius' Apology*. Dissertation, Duke University, Durham, N. C., 1991.

Millar, Fergus, "The World of the Golden Ass," *Journal of Roman Studies* 71 (1981) 63–75.

Oldfather, A., H. W. Canter, B. E. Perry, and K. M. Abbott, *Index Apuleianus*, Middletown: American Philological Association, 1934.

Perry, B. E., "Some Aspects of the Literary Art of Apuleius," *Transactions and Proceedings of the American Philological Association* 54 (1923) 196–227.

———, "The Significance of the Title in Apuleius' *Metamorphoses*," *Classical Philology* 18 (1923) 230–238.

———, "An Interpretation of Apuleius' *Metamorphoses*," *Transactions and Proceedings of the American Philological Association* 57 (1926) 238–260.

———, "On Apuleius' *Met.* I 14–17," *Classical Philology* 24 (1929) 394–400.

———, *The Ancient Romances. A Literary-Historical Account of their Origins*. Berkeley and Los Angeles: University of California Press, 1967.

Sandy, G. N., "Foreshadowing and Suspense in Apuleius' *Metamorphoses*," *Classical Journal* 68 (1972/73) 232–235.

———, "Recent Scholarship on Prose Fiction of Classical Antiquity," *Classical World* 67 (1974) 321–359.

Schlam, C., "The Curiosity of the *Golden Ass*," *Classical Journal* 64 (1968) 120–125.

———, "The Scholarship on Apuleius since 1938," *Classical World* 64 (1971) 285–301.

———, *The* Metamorphoses *of Apuleius. On Making an Ass of Oneself.* Chapel Hill: University of North Carolina Press, 1992.

Scobie, A., "The Confirmation of the Unbelievable in Apuleius' *Metamorphoses*," in: Idem, *More Essays on the Ancient Romance and its Heritage.* Meisenheim am Glan: Verlag Anton Hain, 1973, 35–46.

———, *Apuleius and Folklore.* London: Folklore Society of London, 1983.

Schmeling, Gareth (ed.), *The Novel in the Ancient World.* Leiden-New York-Köln: Brill, 1996 (*Mnemosyne*, Suppl. 159).

Seelinger, R. A., *Magical Motifs in the Metamorphoses of Apuleius.* Dissertation, University of Missouri, Columbia, 1981.

Smith, W. S., "The Narrative Voice in Apuleius' *Metamorphoses*," *Transactions and Proceedings of the American Philological Association* 103 (1972) 513–534.

———, "Style and Character in the Golden Ass: Suddenly an Opposite Appearance," *Aufstieg und Niedergang der römischen Welt* II.34.2 (1994) 1575–1599.

Summers, R. G., "Roman Justice and Apuleius' *Metamorphoses*," *Transactions and Proceedings of the American Philological Association* 101 (1970) 511–531.

———, "Apuleius Juridicus," *Historia* 21 (1972) 120–126.

———, "A note on the date of the *Golden Ass*," *American Journal of Philology* 94 (1973) 375–383.

Tatum, J., "The Tales in Apuleius' *Metamorphoses*," *Transactions and Proceedings of the American Philological Association* 100 (1969) 487–527.

———, "Apuleius and Metamorphosis," *American Journal of Philology* 93 (1972) 306–313.

———, *Apuleius and the* Golden Ass. Ithaca, NY: Cornell University Press, 1979.

Walker, J. M., *The* Satyricon, *the* Golden Ass, *and the Spanish Age Novel.* Dissertation, Brigham Young University, Provo (Utah) 1971.

Walsh, P. G., "Apuleius," in: *The Cambridge History of Classical Literature, vol. II: Latin Literature.* E. J. Kenney, ed. Cambridge, 1982, 774–786.

———, *The Roman Novel : The* Satyricon *of Petronius and the* Metamorphoses *of Apuleius.* Cambridge: the University Press, 1970.

Winkler, J. J., *Auctor & Actor. A Narratological Reading of Apuleius's* The Golden Ass. Berkeley, Los Angeles, and London: University of California Press, 1985.

Wright, C. S., "No Art at All. A Note on the Prooemium of Apuleius' *Metamorphoses*," *Classical Philology* 68 (1973) 217–219.

Glossary

○ ◗ ◖ ● ◗ ○ ○

The glossary below contains the words found in Book 1 of Apuleius' *Metamorphoses*. It is by no means a substitute for a good dictionary; the meanings given are as much as possible specific to the use of the words in this Book. Where the meanings are the subject of discussion, references are sometimes given to comments made in the notes, above, in the form "see 1n," meaning "see the note on section 1." In general, principal parts are given in full: but fully regular first or fourth conjugation verbs are indicated by (1) or (4), respectively. Verbs with infinitives in -ere are third conjugation unless noted ["(2)"]. The following abbreviations are used:

abl.	ablative
acc.	accusative
adj.	adjective
adv.	adverb
conj.	conjunction
dat.	dative
f	feminine
gen.	genitive
imper.	imperative
indef.	indefinite
inf.	infinitive
interj.	interjection
m	masculine
n	neuter
nom.	nominative
pl.	plural
ppp.	perfect passive participle
prep.	preposition
pron.	pronoun
s.	singular
vi.	intransitive verb
vt.	transitive verb

A

a, ab: *prep.* + *abl.*, from, away from; *with passive verb indicating agent*, by

abeo, abire, abii, abitum: *vi.*, go away, depart

abnuo, abnuere, abnui, —: *vi.*, shake one's head, refuse

absolvo, absolvere, absolvi, absolutum: *vt.*, release, open (as for doors, ch. 15, line 274)

absonus, absona, absonum: *adj.*, raucous, discordant

abstinentia, abstinentiae, f: frugality, stinginess

absum, abesse, afui, afuturus: *vi.*, be absent, be away

absurdus, absurda, absurdum: *adj.*, ridiculous, nonsensical

ac, atque: *conj.*, and, and especially. Normally, **ac** is used before consonants, **atque** before vowels, but **atque** is used before "g" in ch. 7, line 131.

accedo, accedere, accessi, accessum: *vi.*, and *vt.*, agree with; go to

accipio, accipere, accepi, acceptum: *vt.*, receive, take, hear

accubo (1): *vt.*, lie on, recline on

accuratius: *comparative adv.*, more closely, more carefully, in more detail

acerbus, acerba, acerbum: *adj.*, harsh, bitter

actum, acti, n: deed, act

ad: *prep.* + *acc.*, toward, at, for; substitute for dative (line 47)

adcurro, adcurrere, adcucurri, adcursum: *vi.*, run, hurry

adduco, adducere, adduxi, adductum: *vt.*, draw, lead, bring, induce, pull shut

adfecto (1): *vt.*, grasp for, try to get, strive for

adfectus, adfecta, adfectum: *adj.*, bothered, disturbed, shaken

adfictus, adficta, adfictum: *adj.*, made up

adgestus, adgesta, adgestum: *adj.*, (*ppp.* < adgero), brought up, pushed up

adhuc: *adv.*, as yet, still, up till now

adiacens, adiacentis: *adj.*, adjoining

adlubentia, adlubentiae, f: willingness, desire

admiratio, admirationis, f: wonder, amazement

admitto, admittere, admisi, admissum: *vt.*, allow

admodum: *adv.*, very

admolior (4): *vt.*, raise, gather, round up

admoveo, admovere (2), admovi, admotum: *vt.*, bring forward, bring up

adnuo, adnuere, adnui, —: *vi.*, nod (yes)

adorior, adoriri, adortus sum: *vi.*, rise, try, undertake

adplico (1): *vt.*, direct ... towards

adquiesco, adquiescere, adquievi, —: *vi.*, find comfort, come to rest

adripio, adripere, adripui, adreptum: *vt.*, grab

adrogo (1): *vt.*, confer ... upon, appropriate

adsido, adsidere, adsedi, adsessum: *vi.*, and *vt.*, sit, sit at

adsolet = solet (see soleo)

adsum, adesse, adfui, adfuturus: *vi.*, be present, be near

adsurgo, adsurgere, adsurrexi, adsurrectum: *vi.*, get up, arise

adtraho, adtrahere, adtraxi, adtractum: *vt.*, drag, pull

adulescentula, adulescentulae, f: young woman

advena, advenae, m: stranger, newcomer

adventor, adventoris, m: visitor, guest

adversus: *prep. + acc.*, against

aedes, aedis, f: house, dwelling

aedificium, aedifcii, n: building

aedilis, aedilis, m: Aedile, a magistrate whose duties included supervising markets

aedilitas, aedilitatis, f: the aedileship, the office of Aedile

Aegiensis, Aegiensis, Aegiense: *adj.*, from Aegeum (in Achaea, see 5n, line 77)

aegre: *adv.*, with difficulty, painfully, reluctantly; *superlative* aegerrime

Aegyptius, Aegyptia, Aegyptium: *adj.*, Egyptian

aemulo (1): *vt.*, imitate, reflect, emulate

aemulus, aemuli, m: rival

aequus, aequa, aequum: *adj.*, fair

aerugo, aeruginis, f: greed, money (lit., the rust on copper)

aerumnabilis, aerumnabilis, aerumnabile: *adj.*, troubled, wretched, miserable

aerumna, aerumnae, f: trouble, tribulation, difficulty

aetas, aetatis, f: age

aetatula, aetatulae, f: youth, tender age

aeternum: adv., forever

aeternus, aeterna, aeternum: *adj.*, permanent, eternal

Aethiopes, Aethiopum, m: Ethiopians

Aetolia, Aetoliae, f: Aetolia, in Greece

affatim: *adv.*, enough

affecto (1): *vt.*, grasp for, strive for

affectus, affectus, m: emotion

aggredior, aggredi, aggressus sum: *vt.*, approach, attack

agilis, agilis, agile: *adj.*, quick

agito (1): *vt.*, occupy oneself with

agnosco, agnoscere, agnovi, agnitum: *vt.*, recognize

ago, agere, egi, actum: *vt.*, do, (lawsuit) plead, conduct

aio, —, —, —: *defective vi.*, say, assert. The forms that appear in this Book are *aio, ais, ait.*

alacer, alacris, alacre: *adj.*, quick, swift

alioquin: *adv.*, in general, basically (see 2n, line 35)

aliquando: *adv.*, eventually, sometimes

aliquantisper: *adv.*, for a little while

aliquanto: *adv.*, (by) a little

aliquantum: *adv.*, a little

aliquis, aliquid (*gen.* alicuius): *indef. adj.*, some (or other); *indef. pron.*, someone, something

alius, alia, alium: *adj.*, other, another

alter, altera, alterum (*gen.* alterius): *adj.*, the other, the second; *used correlatively* (alter ... alter), the one ... the other

altrinsecus: *adv.*, on the other side

altus, alta, altum: *adj.*, high, deep, (of time) late

alvus, alvi, m: belly

amanter: *adv.*, lovingly

amator, amatoris, m: lover

ambages, ambagum, f: riddle, digression

ambulatorius, ambulatoria, ambulatorium: *adj.*, walking, taken on the walk, on the hoof

amicus, amici, m: friend

amnis, amnis, m: stream

amo (1): *vt.*, love; amo, *used colloquially*, I thank (see 22n, line 436)

amor, amoris, m: love

amplector (1): *vt.*, embrace

amplexus, amplexus, m: coil, twist

ampliter: *adv.*, fully

an: *conj.*, or; *introducing alternatives*, whether

ancilla, ancillae, f: slavewoman, slave

ancillula, ancillulae, f: serving girl, slave

angiportus, angiportus, m: lane, alley, side-street

angulus, anguli, m: corner, nook

animus, animi, m: mind, heart

annona, annonae, f: grain supply

annosus, annosa, annosum: *adj.*, full of years, old

annuntio (1): *vt.*, announce

annus, anni, m: year

ante: *prep. + acc.*, before; *adv.*, earlier

antelucium, antelucii, n: the pre-dawn

anteluculum, anteluculi, n: the pre-dawn

antepolleo, antepollere (2), antepollui, —: *vi.*, excel

antevorto, antevortere, antevorti, antevorsum: *vt.*, anticipate, prevent

Anticthones, Anticthonum, m: those dwelling on the other side of the world

anus, anus, f: woman, old woman

anxius, anxia, anxium: *adj.*, concerned, anxious

apage: get ... away! (see 17n, line 325)

appello (1): *vt.*, call to, appeal to

approno (1): *vt.*, lay face down

apud: *prep. + acc.*, with, at the house of, among, in (a city)

aqua, aquae, f: water

arbiter, arbitri, m: examiner, judge

arbitror (1): *vt.*, judge, think, examine (see 18n, line 333)

arduus, ardua, arduum: *adj.*, difficult, hard

arenosus, arenosa, arenosum: *adj.*, sandy

argentum, argenti, n: silver

argutia, argutiae, f: cleverness, dexterity

aries, arietis, m: ram

Aristomenes: the name of the narrator of the tale. (*vocative*, Aristomene; *ablative*, Aristomene).

arrabo, arrabonis, m: security, collateral

arrideo, arridere (2), arrisi, arrisum: *vt.*, laugh (at)

ars, artis, f: art, skill

artius: *comparative adv.*, more closely

ascendo, ascendere, ascendi, ascensum: *vt.*, climb up (on)

aspectus, aspectus, m: sight, appearance

asper, aspera, asperum: *adj.*, harsh, rough, difficult

aspergo, aspergere, aspersi, aspersum: *vt.*, splatter, sprinkle, taint

aspernor (1): *vt.*, turn away (from), reject, despise

aspicio, aspicere, aspexi, aspectum: *vt.*, look at, notice, see

aspritudo, aspritudinis, f: difficulty, steepness

astrictus, astricta, astrictum: *adj.*, tightened

astus, astus, m: cunning, craftiness

at: *conj.*, but, on the contrary, and yet

Athenae, Athenarum, f: Athens

atque = ac

attentus, attenta, attentum: *adj.*, detained, kept busy

Atticus, Attica, Atticum: *adj.,* from Attica, the area around Athens

attingo, attingere, attigi, attectum: *vt.,* touch

Attis, Attidis: *adj.,* Athenian, Attic, Greek

attonitus, attonita, attonitum: *adj.,* stunned

auctor, auctoris, m: instigator

audio (4): *vt.,* hear

auditu: *supine, abl. of respect,* hearing, to hear

aufero, auferre, abstuli, ablatum: *vt.,* take away, carry away

aufugio, aufugere, aufugi, aufugitum: *vi.,* run away, flee

aulaeum, aulaei, n: curtain

aures, auris, f: ear

aurum, auri, n: gold

ausculto (1): *vt.,* listen

autem: *conj.,* however, moreover, on the other hand

autumo (1): *vt.,* assert, affirm, maintain

avaritia, avaritiae, f: greed

avello, avellere, avulsi, avulsum: *vt.,* tear away, tear out

avide: *adv.,* greedily, eagerly

avidus, avida, avidum: *adj.,* greedy, eager

avius, avia, avium: *adj.,* uncharted, unknown, pathless

avoco (1): *vt.,* divert, distract, call away

B

bacchatim: *adv.,* in a frenzy, like a Bacchant

bacillum, bacilli, n: little stick, staff

baculum, baculi, n: staff, rod

balbuttio (4): *vi.,* stammer, babble

balneae, balnearum, f: baths

bene: *adv.,* fine; *intensive,* quite

beneficium, beneficii, n: kindness, favor

benigne: *adv.,* kindly

benivolus, benivola, benivolum: *adj.,* kind

bestia, bestiae, f: beast

biduum, bidui, n: a period of two days

Boeotia, Boeotiae, f: Boeotia, in eastern Greece

bonus, bona, bonum: *adj.,* good, kindly

breviculus, brevicula, breviculum: *adj.,* rather short

brevitas, brevitatis, f: smallness

buxeus, buxea, buxeum: *adj.,* yellowish

C

cachinnus, cachinni, m: cackle, laughter

caedes, caedis, f: murder

caelum, caeli, n: sky

caespes, caespitis, m: turf, grass

calamitas, calamitatis, f: disaster

calamus, calami, m: reed, reed pen

calleo, callere (2), callui, —: *vi.,* to be clever

calumnior (1): *vt.,* claim falsely, slander

Calypso, Calypsonis, f: name of the divine captor of Odysseus on Ogygia (see 12n, line 223)

campus, campi, m: plain, field

candidatus, candidati, m: candidate

canis, canis, m: dog

cantio, cantionis, f: incantation, spell

capesso, capessere, capessivi, capessitum: *vt.,* lay hold of, snatch at, grab

capio, capere, cepi, captum: *vt.*, catch, grab, get

captivitas, captivitatis, f: enslavement, capture

captus, captus, m: grasp, catching

capulus, capuli, m: handle, hilt

caput, capitis, n: head

cardo, cardinis, m: hinge, socket

caritas, caritatis, f: dearness, high price, costliness

carus, cara, carum: *adj.*, dear

caseatus, caseata, caseatum: *adj.*, made of cheese

caseum, casei, n: cheese

castor, castoris, m: beaver

casus, casus, m: fall, mishap

Catamitus, Catamiti, m: Ganymedes (see 12n, line 220)

caupo, cauponis, m: innkeeper

caupona, cauponae, f: inn, innkeeper

causa, causae, f: cause, reason, case (in court)

cave: *imper. vt.*, take care, be sure; = *noli*, don't ... (*followed by the subjunctive without* ne)

cavillum, cavilli, n: banter

cedo: *imper.*, give (see 4n, line 67)

celeritas, celeritatis, f: speed

cena, cenae, f: dinner, meal

cenatus, cenata, cenatum: *adj.*, provided with dinner

ceno (1): *vt.*, eat, dine

censeo, censere (2), censui, censum: *vt.*, think, consider

centesimus, centesima, centesimum: *adj.*, hundredth

centum: *indeclinable adj.*, hundred

centunculus, centunculi, m: rag cloak

Cerberus, Cerberi, m: name of the three-headed dog who guards the underworld

cernuo (1): *vi.*, fall head first

certe: *adv.*, surely, definitely, at least

ceteri, ceterae, cetera: *adj.*, the rest (of)

cibatus, cibatus, m: eating

cibus, cibi, m: food

cicatrix, cicatricis, f: scar

circa: *prep. + acc.*, around

circulator, circulatoris, m: wandering performer

circumspicio, circumspicere, circumspexi, circumspectum: *vt.*, look around (at)

circumsto, circumstare, circumsteti, circumstatum: *vi.*, stand around, stand over

cito (1): call, name

citro: *adv.*, on the near side

civitas, civitatis, f: city

clamito (1): *vi.*, shout out

clamor, clamoris, m: uproar, shouting

claudo, claudere, clausi, clausum: *vt.*, close, shut

claustra, claustrorum, n: bolts

clavis, clavis, f: key

clementer: *adv.*, mildly, calmly

Clytius, Clytii, m: name of Lucius' and Pythias' teacher in Athens

coemo, coemere, coemi, coemptum: *vt.*, buy

coepi, coepisse, coeptum: *vt.*, (perfect system only) began

coerceo, coercere (2), coercui, coercitum: *vt.*, compel

coetus, coetus, m: assembly

cogitatio, cogitationis, f: thinking, thought

cogito (1): *vt.*, think, ponder

cognitor, cognitoris, m: one who knows

cognomen, cognominis, n: name, cognomen

cognosco, cognoscere, cognovi, cognitum: *vt.*, know, recognize

cogo, cogere, coegi, coactum: *vt.*, compel, force

colligo (1): *vt.*, bind together, constrain

collustro (1): *vt.*, bathe in light

colo, colere, colui, cultum: *vt.*, live in, dwell in, study, perfect

color, coloris, m: color

comes, comitis, m: companion

comiter: *adv.*, gently, kindly, in a friendly way

comitor (1): *vt.*, accompany

commeo (1): *vt.*, go along with, accompany

commodo (1): *vt.*, help, assist

commodum: *adv.*, merely, only (see 5n, line 86)

commodus, commoda, commodum: *adj.*, comfortable, agreeable

communis, communis, commune: *adj.*, common (shared), ordinary

compareo, comparere (2), comparui, —: *vi.*, appear

comparo (1): *vt.*, get, buy

compello, compellere, compuli, compulsum: *vt.*, induce, pressure

compendium, compendii, n: profit

compertus, comperta, compertum: *adj.*, (*ppp.* < comperio) discovered, found out

compertus, compertus, m: a discovering

complicitus, complicita, complicitum: *adj.*, (*ppp.* < complico), (having) bent, folded

complico, complicare, complicui, complicitum: *vt.*, fold up

concedo, concedere, concessi, concessum: *vi.*, go away, go off

concilio (1): *vt.*, recommend, bring together

conclamo (1): *vi.*, shout out

condiscipulus, condiscipuli, m: fellow student

condo, condere, condidi, conditum: *vt.*, store, put away, preserve; stick (of a sword)

confero, conferre, contuli, conlatum: *vt.*, turn over, give up

confestim: *adv.*, right away, without delay

congressus, congressus, m: intercourse

congruens, congruentis: *adj.*, agreeing with, matching

conicio, conicere, conieci, coniectum: *vt.*, guess

coniveo, conivere (2), conivi, —: *vi.*, close one's eyes

conscius, conscia, conscium: *adj.*, feeling guilty, self-conscious, complicit

consector (1): follow, pursue, overtake

consero, conserere, conserui, consertum: *vt.*, stitch together, connect, entwine

consiliator, consiliatoris, m: advisor

consilium, consilii, n: advice, counsel, effort

consone: *adv.*, in harmony, all together

conspectus, conspectus, m: view, vision

conspicio, conspicere, conspexi, conspectum: *vt.*, notice, see, catch sight of

conspicor (1): *vt.*, notice, see, catch sight of

consternatus, consternata, consternatum: *adj.*, upset, bothered, taken aback

consulo, consulere, consului, consultum: *vt.*, advise, discuss

contego, contegere, contexi, contectum: *vt.*, cover

contentus, contenta, contentum: *adj.*, satisfied, content

contineo, continere (2), continui, contentum: *vt.*, hold back

continor (1): *vt.*, encounter

contraho, contrahere, contraxi, contractum: *vt.*, get, incur, acquire

contrarium, contrarii, n: the opposite

contrunco (1): *vt.*, hack up, chop up; devour, gobble (food)

contubernalis, contubernalis, m: room-mate, old friend

contumelia, contumeliae, f: outrage, verbal abuse, punishment

contumulo (1): *vt.*, pile up, bury

convallis, convallis, f: hamlet

convector, convectoris, m: fellow traveler

convenio, convenire, conveni, conventum: *vi.*, correspond to, fit with, agree with

converto, convertere, converti, conversum: *vt.*, turn, change

conviva, convivae, m: guest

convivium, convivii, n: party

cooperio, cooperire, cooperui, coopertum: *vt.*, cover over

copiosus, copiosa, copiosum: *adj.*, abundant

cor, cordis, n: heart

Corinthius, Corinthia, Corinthium: *adj.*, from Corinth (a Greek city)

coronalis, coronalis, coronale: *adj.*, from a crown, on the head

corpus, corporis, n: body

crapula, crapulae, f: drunkenness, intoxication

crassus, crassa, crassum: *adj.*, thick, deaf

crastinus, crastina, crastinum: *adj.*, tomorrow's, of tomorrow

creber, crebra, crebrum: *adj.*, repeated, frequent

crebritas, crebritatis, f: density, frequency

crebriter: *adv.*, constantly

credo, credere, credidi, creditum: *vi.*, believe, trust; *the word* credo ("I suppose") *is often used to display sarcasm, irony, or scorn*

Creo and **Creon, Creonis,** m: Creon, a king of Athens (see 10n, line 175)

cruciabilis, cruciabilis, cruciabile: *adj.*, painful, torturous

crudelitas, crudelitatis, f: cruelty

cruor, cruoris, m: blood, gore

crux, crucis, f: cross, torture

cubiculum, cubiculi, n: room, bedroom

cubile, cubilis, n: bed, resting place

cubito (1): customarily lie

cubitum: *supine of purpose*, to go to bed

cucurbita, cucurbitae, f: gourd

cuias, cuiatis: *adj.*, from what country

cum: *conj.*, when, because, since, although

cum: *prep. + abl.*, with, accompanied by, at the same time as (*in the phrase* et cum dicto)

cumulo (1): *vt.*, pile up

cuncti, cunctae, cuncta: *adj.*, all

cunctor (1): *vi.*, hesitate

cupido, cupidinis, m: desire

cupio, cupere, cupivi, cupitum: *vt.*, wish, want

cur: *adv.*, why

curiose: *adv.*, carefully, closely, with curiosity

curiositas, curiositatis, f: curiosity

curiosus, curiosa, curiosum: *adj.*, inquisitive, nosey, curious

curo (1): *vt.*, be in charge of, care for, take care of

D

damno (1): *vt.*, condemn

de: *prep.* + *abl.*, from, down from, of, from, about

debeo, debere (2), debui, debitum: *vi.*, ought, must

decedo, decedere, decessi, decessum: *vi.*, depart

decem: *indeclinable adj.*, ten

decermina, decerminum, n: decisions, decrees

decerno, decernere, decrevi, decretum: *vt.*, decide, determine, decree

decimus, decima, decimum: *adj.*, tenth

decorus, decora, decorum: *adj.*, beautiful

decretum, decreti, n: decree, decision

dedecus, dedecoris, n: disgrace

deduco, deducere, deduxi, deductum: *vt.*, reduce, bring down

deductus, deductus, m: downward pull

deficio, deficere, defeci, defectum: *vi.*, be (made) weak, be inadequate, fail

defleo, deflere (2), deflevi, defletum: *vt.*, bewail, lament

deformo (1): *vt.*, transform, turn ... (into)

dehinc: *adv.*, after that, from here

dehisco, dehiscere, —, —: *vi.*, gape open, yawn

deicio, deicere, dieci, deiectum: *vt.*, cast down

deiero (1): *vt.*, swear (an oath)

dein: *adv.*, then, next

deinde: *adv.*, then, next

delabor, delabi, delapsus sum: *vt.*, slip in (sword)

delibero (1): ponder

Demeas, Demeae, m: name of one of Lucius's friends; *acc.* Demean

demeo (1): *vi.*, move (downward)

demergo, demergere, demersi, demersum: *vt.*, submerge, overwhelm, plunge

demonstro (1): show, illustrate, point to

demuto (1): change, alter, detract

denarii, denariorum (or denarium), m: denarii (a measure of Roman money, equivalent to four sesterces)

denique: *adv.*, for example, finally, lastly, in short

densus, densa, densum: *adj.*, thick, crowded

denuo: *adv.*, anew, again

deorsum: *adv.*, down(ward)

deosculor (1): *vt.*, kiss (with feeling)

depono, deponere, deposui, depositum: *vt.*, push down, put down

derivo (1): *vt.*, channel, change the direction of

deseco (1): cut off

desertus, deserta, desertum: *adj.*, abandoned

desidero (1): *vt.*, want, need

desilio (4): *vi.*, leap down

desino, desinere, desivi, desitum: *vt.*, stop, leave off

despolior (1): *vt.*, loot, get the spoils from

despumor (1): *vt.*, draw the foam from

destinatus, destinata, destinatum: *adj.*, tied up, made fast desultorius, desultoria, desultorium: *adj.*, of leaping (from one horse to another; see 1n, line 15)

detestor (1): *vt.*, malign, slander

detorqueo, detorquere (2), detorsi, detortum: *vt.*, twist

detraho, detrahere, detraxi, detractum: *vt.*, pull away, pull down

detrunco (1): *vt.*, mutilate, behead; devour (food)

deuro, deurere, deussi, deustum: *vt.*, burn completely

deus, dei, m: god

deversor, deversari, deversus sum: *vi.*, live, stay, dwell

devolvor, devolvi, devulsus sum: *vi.*, roll out

devoro (1): *vt.*, swallow down, devour

devorto, devortere, devorti, devorsum: *vi.*, stay (for the night), turn aside, stop in

devotio, devotionis, f: solemn vow

dexter, dextera (or dextra), dextrum: *adj.*, right

dicacitas, dicacitatis, f: wit, joking

dicacule: *adv.*, wittily

dico, dicere, dixi, dictum: *vt.*, say, tell; *dicto: et cum dicto* (see 6n, line 103)

diecula, dieculae, f: (little) day

dies, diei, m/f: day, daylight

diffamo (1): *vt.*, slander

diffleo, difflere (2), difflevi, diffletum: *vt.*, weep to exhaustion

digitus, digiti, m: finger

dignatio, dignationis, f: reputation, stature

dignus, digna, dignum: *adj.*, worth, worthy

digredior, digredi, digressus sum: *vi.*, leave, depart

diligenter: *adv.*, carefully

diluo, diluere, dilui, dilutum: *vt.*, wash away

dimoveo, dimovere (2), dimovi, dimotum: *vt.*, remove, set aside, turn aside

dirumpo, dirumpere, dirupi, diruptum: *vt.*, burst apart

dirus, dira, dirum: *adj.*, dreadful, dangerous

discedo, discedere, discessi, discessum: *vi.*, leave, go away

discerpo, discerpere, discerpsi, discerptum: *vt.*, pull apart

discludo, discludere, discludi, disclusum: *vt.*, shut off, cut off

discurro, discurrere, discurri, discursum: *vi.*, run around

discutio, discutere, discussi, discussum: *vt.*, dispel, disperse

distendo, distendere, distendi, distentum: *vt.*, bloat

distineo, distinere (2), distinui, distentum: block, obstruct, hinder, occupy

distraho, distrahere, distraxi, distractum: *vt.*, sell in parcels

diu: *adv.*, a long time; *comparative* diutius, a longer time

diuturnus, diuturna, diuturnum: *adj.*, long lasting

diversus, diversa, diversum: *adj.*, different, various

divinus, divina, divinum: *adj.*, divine

do, dare, dedi, datum: *vt.*, give

doleo, dolere (2), dolui, dolitum: *vi.*, be in pain, hurt

dolium, dolii, n: vat

domuitio, domuitionis, f: returning home, homecoming

domus, domus, f: house, home; *locative*, domi, at home

dorsum, dorsi, n: back
dubito (1): *vt.,* doubt
dubius, dubia, dubium: *adj.,* doubtful
duco, ducere, duxi, ductum: *vt.,* bring, lead
dudum: *adv.,* formerly, a while ago
dum: *conj.,* while
duo, duae, duo: *adj.,* two
duro (1): *vt.,* harden, solidify

e

e, ex: *prep. + abl.,* from, out of, straight from
ebrius, ebria, ebrium: *adj.,* drunk
ecce: *interj.,* look, behold
edo, edere, edidi, editum: *vt.,* issue, proclaim
edulia, edulium, n: foodstuffs, things to eat
efficio, efficere, effeci, effectum: *vt.,* cause, make
efflictim: *adv.,* desperately
effrico (1): *vt.,* scrape ... from
effundo, effundere, effudi, effusum: *vt.,* pour out ... from
egredior, egredi, egressus sum: *vi.,* leave, go out
elephantus, elephanti, m: elephant
eliquo (1): *vt.,* remove, filter out
eluvies, eluviei, f: flood, flow
emergo, emergere, emersi, emersum: *vi.,* rise up, get up, disentangle oneself
emo, emere, emi, emptum: *vt.,* buy
en: *interj.,* look, behold
Endymion: name of the beloved of the moon-goddess in myth; see 12n, line 220
enervus, enerva, enervum: *adj.,* muscle-less, pliant

enim: *conj.,* because, for, in fact
enitor, eniti, enisus sum: *vi.,* struggle, strive
enormis, enormis, enorme: *adj.,* huge, immense
eo, ire, ii (ivi), itum: *vi.,* go
Ephyreus, Ephyrea, Ephyreum: *adj.,* of Corinth, Corinthian
equester, equestris, equestre: *adj.,* belonging to a horseman, knight's
equidem: *adv.,* indeed, certainly, to be sure
equus, equi, m: horse
ergo: *conj.,* for this reason, therefore
erogo (1): *vt.,* prevail upon, obtain by pleading
eruptio, eruptionis, f: spurt, gush
erus, eri, m: master
essito (1): *vt.,* gobble, eat
esurio (4): *vi.,* be hungry
et: *conj.,* and; *adv.,* even, also
etiam: *adv.,* also, even
etsi: *conj.,* even if
evado, evadere, evasi, evasum: *vt.* and *vi.,* escape, get away from
evello, evellere, evolsi, evolsum: *vt.,* tear out, root out, remove
evidens, evidentis: *adj.,* plain, clear
evolvo, evolvere, evolvi, evolutum: *vt.,* roll out
exanclo (1): *vt.,* suffer, go through (see 16n, line 296)
exanimatus, exanimata, exanimatum: *adj.,* lifeless
exasperatus, exasperata, exasperatum: *adj.,* quite rugged
excipio, excipere, excepi, exceptum: *vt.,* catch
excolo, excolere, excolui, excultum: *vt.,* work at, perfect
excuso (1): decline, say no, make one's excuses

excutio, excutere, excussi,
  excussum: *vt.*, shake out
exerceo, exercere (2), exercui,
  exercitum: *vt.*, practice, engage
  in
exiguus, exigua, exiguum: *adj.*,
  small, overly small
exilium, exilii, n: exile
eximie: *adv.*, extremely, very
exinde: *adv.*, from the time
exitium, exitii, n: destruction,
  death
exonero (1): *vt.*, relieve, unburden
exordior, exordiri, exortus sum: *vt.*,
  begin
exortus, exortus, m: rising,
  emergence
exossus, exossa, exossum: *adj.*,
  bone-less
exoticus, exotica, exoticum: *adj.*,
  strange, foreign
expedio (4): *vt.*, disentangle, set
  free
expergiscor, expergisci,
  experrectus sum: *vi.*, wake up,
  get up
expleo, explere (2), explevi,
  expletum: *vt.*, fill
explico (1): unfold
exploro (1): investigate
expono, exponere, exposui,
  expositum: lay out, display
exserte: *adv.*, at the top of his voice,
  loudly
exsertus, exserta, exsertum: *adj.*,
  pushed out, uncovered
exspiro (1): *vt.*, breathe out
exstinguo, exstinguere, exstingui,
  exstinctum: *vt.*, put out, douse
exsurgo, exsurgere, esurrexi,
  esurrectum: *vi.*, get up, arise
extorqueo, extorquere (2), extorsi,
  extorsum: *vt.*, get by force,
  extort, wrest away
extra: *prep. + acc.*, outside

extremus, extrema, extremum:
  superlative adj., farthest part
  of, bottom of, top of, tip of,
  farthest, extreme; *used as a*
  substantive, remotest parts;
  comparative: extremius (see 8n,
  line 140).
exuo, exuere, exui, exutum: *vt.*, take
  off

Ғ

fabula, fabulae, f: story, fable
fabulosus, fabulosa, fabulosum:
  fantastic, fictional
facies, faciei, f: face
facile: *adv.*, easily
facilis, facilis, facile: *adj.*, easy
facinus, facinoris, n: crime
facio, facere, feci, factum: make,
  do, perform, deem, see to it
  (that); factu: *supine, abl. of*
  respect, to do; *archaic future*
  perfect, faxo (see 12n, line 229)
faenum, faeni, n: hay
faenus, faenoris, n: money-
  lending
faex, faecis, f: muck, slop
famelicus, famelica, famelicum:
  adj., hungry, without food
famigerabilis, famigerabilis,
  famigerabile: *adj.*, famous,
  renowned
fata, fatorum, n: fate, the fates
fatigatio, fatigationis, f: weariness
fatigatus, fatigata, fatigatum: *adj.*,
  worn out
fauces, faucium, f: throat
faxo: see *facio* and 12n, line 229
felix, felicis: *adj.*, happy, fertile
femina, feminae, f: woman
fenestra, fenestrae, f: window
fera, ferae, m/f: wild animal,
  beast
ferme: *adv.*, nearly

fero, ferre, tuli, latum: *vt.*, bring, bear
ferrum, ferri, n: iron, metal
fessus, fessa, fessum: *adj.*, tired, weary
festino (1): *vi.*, hurry
festinus, festina, festinum: *adj.*, quick, in a hurry
festivitas, festivitatis, f: charm, fun, humor
fetor, fetoris, m: stench
fetus, fetus, m: baby
fidelis, fidelis, fidele: *adj.*, loyal
fidens, fidentis: *adj.*, confident, bold
fides, fidei, f: trust, credulity, care
fidus, fida, fidum: *adj.*, trustworthy, loyal, trusting
figo, figere, fixi, fictum: *vt.*, set up, plant
figura, figurae, f: shape, form
filia, filiae, f: daughter
fimum, fimi, n: dung, dirt
finis, finis, m: end
fio, fieri, factus sum: *vi.*, become, be made
firmiter: *adv.*, firmly, tightly
firmo (1): *vt.*, strengthen
flagitium, flagitii, n: outrage, shameful treatment
flamma, flammae, f: flame, fire
fleo, flere (2), flevi, fletum: *vt.*, cry (for)
flexus, flexus, m: twist, bend
flos, floris, m: flower
flumen, fluminis, n: river, stream
fluvius, fluvii, m: stream
folia, foliorum, n: leaves
fons, fontis, m: fountain
foramen, foraminis, n: bolt hole
forensis, forensis, forense: *adj.*, of the forum
foris: *adv.*, outside
foris, foris, f: doorpost, door, leaf of a double door

formido, formidinis, m: fear
forsitan: *adv.*, perhaps
forte: *adv.*, by chance
fortiter: *adv.*, strongly, loudly
fortuna, fortunae, f: fortune, luck
forum, fori, n: forum, marketplace
Fotis, Fotis, f: name of Milo's female slave (see 23n, line 453)
fractus, fracta, fractum: *adj.*, broken
frater, fratris, m: brother
freni, frenorum, m: reins
frigidus, frigida, frigidum: *adj.*, cold
frivolus, frivola, frivolum: *adj.*, trifling, worthless
frons, frontis, f: forehead
fruor, frui, fructus sum: *vi.*, enjoy
frustro (1): *vt.*, disappoint, deceive
frustulum, frustuli, n: little piece, scrap
fuga, fugae, f: flight
fulcimentum, fulcimenti, n: prop
fumus, fumi, m: smoke
fundamentum, fundamenti, n: origin, root, foundation
funditus: *adv.*, deeply
funiculus, funiculi, m: rope, cord
funis, funis, m: rope
Furiae, Furiarum, f: the Furies, (evil) spirits
furtim: *adv.*, stealthily

G

gaudeo, gaudere (2), gavisus sum: *vi.*, rejoice
gaudium, gaudii, n: joy
geminus, gemina, geminum: *adj.*, twin, double
generosus, generosa, generosum: *adj.*, noble

genitalia, genitalium, n: genitals

genua, genuum, n: knees

genus, generis, n: kind, sort

gero, gerere, gessi, gestum: *vt.*, do, carry; serve as (aedile)

gestio (4): *vt.*, desire, long (to)

gladiatorius, gladiatoria, gladiatorium: *adj.*, involving gladiators, gladiatorial

gladius, gladii, m: sword

gleba, glebae, f: clod of dirt

glebosus, glebosa, glebosum: *adj.*, lumpy, clod-filled

gloria, gloriae, f: renown, glory

gloriosus, gloriosa, gloriosum: *adj.*, glorious, excellent

glutinosus, glutinosa, glutinosum: *adj.*, gluey

grabatulus, grabatuli, m: bed, couch

gradus, gradus, m: step, pace

Graecanicus, Graecanica, Graecanicum: *adj.*, Greekish

grandis, grandis, grande: *adj.*, large

gratia, gratiae, f: favor, advantage; *pl.*, thanks

gratuitus, gratuita, gratuitum: *adj.*, without cost, free

gratus, grata, gratum: *adj.*, welcome, grateful

gravatus, gravata, gravatum: *adj.*, weighed down, burdened

gravis, gravis, grave: *adj.*, heavy, serious

gula, gulae, f: throat

gurgustiolus, gurgustioli, m: little hovel

H

habeo, habere (2), habui, habitum: *vt.*, have

habitudo, habitudinis, f: appearance, bearing, attitude

habitus, habitus, m: dress, attitude

haud: *adv.*, not

Hecale, Hecales, f: name of Milo's wife (see 23n, line 452)

hem: *interj.*, well, see here now, say ...

hercule (or hercules): *interj.*, by Hercules

heus: *interj.*, hey!

hic: *adv.*, here

hic, haec, hoc: *demonstrative adj. or pron.*, this; he, she, it

hilaro (1): *vt.*, cheer up, gladden

hoc: *adv.*, (= *huc*), to this place, this way

homo, hominis, m: man, person

honestus, honesta, honestum: *adj.*, honorable, worthy

hora, horae, f: hour

hordeum, hordei, n: barley

hortatio, hortationis, f: pleading

hospes, hospitis, m: guest

hospitium, hospitii, n: hospitality, home, place to stay

humane: *adv.*, kindly, decently

humanus, humana, humanum: *adj.*, human, of a person

humerus, humeri, m: shoulder

humor, humoris, m: liquid

humus, humi, f: ground, earth; *locative* humi, on the ground

Hymettos (*nom. s.*): Hymettus, a mountain range near Athens (see 1n, line 7)

Hypata, Hypatae, f: Hypata, the name of a Thessalian town (see 5n, line 80)

I

iaceo, iacere (2), iacui, —: *vi.*, lie, be located

iacio, iacere, ieci, iactum: *vt.*, contribute, throw out

iacto (1): *vt.*, bandy about, vaunt

iaculatio, iaculationis, f: throw, casting, pelting

iam: *conj.*, now, by now, already; iam dudum: for a long time now

ianitor, ianitoris, m: door-keeper

ianua, ianuae, f: door

ibi: *adv.*, there

ibidem: *adv.*, in the same place

idem, eadem, idem: *emphatic pron.*, same, the same; see also 9n, line 166

identidem: *adv.*, repeatedly, again and again

ientaculum, ientaculi, n: breakfast, meal

igitur: *conj.*, therefore

ignarus, ignari, m: an uneducated person, an ignorant person

ignavus, ignava, ignavum: *adj.*, lazy

ignoro (1): *vt.*, not know, be unaware

ilico: *adv.*, thereupon, on the spot

ille, illa, illud: *demonstrative adj. or pron.*, that; he, she, it

illic: *adv.*, there

illo: *adv.*, (to) there

illudo, illudere, illusi, illusum: *vt.*, play with, trifle with

illumino (1): *vt.*, fill with light

imaginor (1): *vt.*, imagine, fantasize

imago, imaginis, f: image, vision, apparition

immanis, immanis, immane: *adj.*, huge

immerito: *adv.*, without reason, unjustly

immissio, immissionis, f: insertion

immitto, immittere, immisi, immissum: *vt.*, insert, send in

immo: *adv.*, on the contrary, or indeed (to mark an emphatic or additional point, see 153)

immodice: *adv,* immoderately, without restraint

immutatio, immutationis, f: change

impatienter: *adv.*, impatiently

imperium, imperii, n: power

impertio (4): *vt.*, share

impetro (1): *vt.*, get, acquire, obtain

impetus, impetus, m: attack, impact

impio (1): defile, pollute

importune: *adv.*, rudely

impossibilis, impossibilis, impossibile: *adj.*, impossible

impulsus, impulsus, m: attack, assault

impune: *adv.*, without punishment

imus, ima, imum: *adj.*, bottom of, lowest part of

in: *prep. + abl.*, in, within, among; *prep. + acc.*, into, at, for, against

inanimis, inanimis, inanime: *adj.*, lifeless

incedo, incedere, incessi, incessum: *vi.*, walk, go around

incertus, incerta, incertum: *adj.*, vague, undefined

incessus, incessus, m: walk, stroll

incido, incidere, incidi, —: *vi.*, stumble into

incipio, incipere, incepi, inceptum: *vt.*, begin

inclitus, inclita, inclitum: *adj.*, famous

includo, includere, inclusi, inclusum: *vt.*, shut up, enclose

incoho (1): *vt.*, start

incola, incolae, m: inhabitant

incolumis, incolumis, incolume: *adj.*, safe

incommodum, incommodi, n: discomfort

incredulitas, incredulitatis, f: skepticism, disbelief

increpo (1): scold

incursio, incursionis, f: onslaught

incutio, incutere, incussi,
   incussum: *vt.*, instil
inde: *adv.*, then, next, thereupon,
   from there
Indi, Indorum, m: Indians
indicium, indicii, n: charge,
   allegation
indico (1): *vt.*, value, put a price on
indidem: *adv.*, from there, next
indigena, indigenae: *adj.*, native
   (see 1n, line 11)
indigeo, indigere (2), indigui, —:
   vi., want, need
indignatio, indignationis, f: anger,
   outrage
induo, induere, indui, indutum: *vt.*,
   put on
indutiae, indutiarum, f: truce
inefficax, inefficacis: *adj.*, useless
ineptus, inepta, ineptum: *adj.*,
   clumsy, foolish
infamis, infamis, infame: *adj.*, of
   low reputation, unspeakable
infectus, infecta, infectum: *adj.*,
   unprecedented, never done
   before
inferi, inferorum, m: the
   underworld
inferialis, inferialis, inferiale: *adj.*,
   funereal
infero, inferre, intuli, illatum: *vt.*,
   take ... in
infesto (1) *vt.*, overrun, take over,
   crowd
infestus, infesta, infestum: *adj.*,
   awful, ferocious
inficio, inficere, infeci, infectum:
   vt., soak, imbue
infimo (1): *vt.*, bring down
infimus, infima, infimum: *adj.*,
   low, base, contemptible
infit: *vi.*, begins
infortunium, infortunii, n:
   misfortune
ingluvies, ingluviei, f: gullet, throat

ingratis: *adv.*, against one's will
ingressus, ingressus, m: walking
   into, entering
inhabitantes, inhabitantium, m:
   residents
inhaereo, inhaerere (2), inhaesi,
   inhaesum: *vi.*, stick (in), be
   stuck
inhibeo, inhibere, inhibui,
   inhibitum: *vt.*, hold back
inibi: *adv.*, in there
inicio, inicere, inieci,
   iniectum: *vt.*, insert, throw
   over, throw on
initium, initii, n: beginning
innato (1): *vi.*, swim (in)
innocentia, innocentiae, f:
   innocence
inquam, —, —: *vi.*, say (always in
   direct quotations; 3rd person
   form is *inquit*)
inquietus, inquieta, inquietum:
   adj., noisy
inquiro, inquirere, inquisivi,
   inquisitum: *vt.*, ask, explore
inscendo, inscendere, inscendi,
   inscensum: *vt.*, climb on, step
   up on
inscriptus, inscripta, inscriptum:
   adj., (*ppp.* < inscribo), written
   (upon)
insequentes, insequentium, m:
   pursuers
insolitus, insolita, insolitum: *adj.*,
   unusual
insperatus, insperata, insperatum:
   adj., unexpected, unhoped-for
inspicio, inspicere, inspexi,
   inspectum: *vt.*, examine
instabilis, instabilis, instabile: *adj.*,
   unpredictable, unstoppable
instans, instantis: *adj.*, present,
   current
instar, n: *indeclinable noun*,
   likeness, image

instruo, instruere, instruxi, instructum: *vt.*, prepare, arrange

insuper: *adv.*, on top

insurgo, insurgere, insurrexi, insurrectum: *vt.*, go up, climb up; *vi.*, get up

integer, integra, integrum: *adj.*, whole, sound, well, undamaged

intemperans, intemperantis: *adj.*, careless, unrestrained

intempestus, intempesta, intempestum: *adj.*, timeless, where time is unknowable

intendo, intendere, intendi, intentum: *vt.*, pay attention

intentio, intentionis, f: attention, interest

intentus, intenta, intentum: *adj.*, attentive, anxious, focused (on)

intereo, interire, interii, interitum: *vi.*, die

interviso, intervisere, intervisi, intervisum: *vt.*, visit

intextus, intexta, intextum: *adj.*, tied together

intimidus, intimida, intimidum: *adj.*, fearless

intra: *prep. + acc.*, inside, within

intro: *adv.*, within, inside

introrumpo, introrumpere, introrupi, introruptum: *vt.*, burst in, break in

invado, invadere, invasi, invasum: *vt.*, rush upon, happen to meet

invenio, invenire, inveni, inventum: *vt.*, find, discover

inversus, inversa, inversum: *adj.*, upside-down, turned around

invitamentum, invitamenti, n: inducement

involutus, involuta, involutum: *adj.*, wrapped up

iocus, ioci, m: joke, joking

ipse, ipsa, ipsum: *intensive adj. or pron.*, himself, herself, itself, the very

irrumpo, irrumpere, irrupi, irruptum: *vt.*, break in, burst in

is, ea, id: *demonstrative adj. or pron.*, this, that; he, she, it

iste, ista, istud = *ille, illa, illud*

Isthmos (*nom. singular*): the Isthmus of Corinth (see 1n, lines 7–8)

istic: *adv.*, there

istinc: *adv.*, from there

ita: *adv.*, thus, in this way, so

itaque: *conj.*, and so, therefore

iter, itineris, n: journey, trip

iubar, iubaris, n: sun-beam(s)

iubeo, iubere (2), iussi, iussum: *vt.*, ask, order, bid

iucunditas, iucunditatis, f: amiability, affability

iugulo (1): *vt.*, cut the throat, murder

iugulum, iuguli, n: neck, throat

iugum, iugi, n: ridge

iuridicus, iuridici, m: (provincial) judge

ius iurandum, iuris iurandi, n: oath

iuxta: *prep. + acc.*, next to

L

labium, labii, n: lip

labor, laboris, m: trouble, toil, difficulty

lacinia, laciniae, f: fold, flap, hem; garment (*in plural and by metonymy*)

lacrima, lacrimae, f: tear, teardrop

lacteus, lactea, lacteum: *adj.*, milky white

lacunosus, lacunosa, lacunosum: *adj.*, full of holes

laetor (1): *vi.*, be glad, rejoice

laetus, laeta, laetum: *adj.*, happy

laevorsum: *adv.*, to the left

lamia, lamiae, f: witch

lancea, lanceae, f: spear

lapis, lapidis, m: stone, milestone

laqueus, laquei, m: noose

Lar, Laris, m: Lar, or Roman household god; by metonymy = home

Larissa, Larissae, f: a city in Thessaly

larvalis, larvalis, larvale: *adj.*, ghostly, like a ghost

lassitudo, lassitudinis, f: weariness

lassus, lassa, lassum: *adj.*, worn out, tired out

latex, laticis, m: liquid, water

Latius, Latia, Latium: *adj.*, of Latium

latrina, latrinae, f: latrine

latro, latronis, m: robber

latrocinium, latrocinii, n: crime, robbery

latus, lateris, n: side

lautus, lauta, lautum: *adj.* (*ppp.* < lavo), clean, having bathed

lavacrum, lavacri, n: public bath

lector, lectoris, m: reader

lectulus, lectuli, m: (little) bed

lego, legere, legi, lectum: *vt.*, read

lenis, lenis, lene: *adj.*, gentle, slow

lepidus, lepida, lepidum: *adj.*, charming, delightful, clever

levigo (1): *vt.*, lighten, relieve

levo (1): *vt.*, lighten, relieve

libenter: *adv.*, gladly

liber, libri, m: book

liberi, liberorum, m: children

libero (1): *vt.*, free

licet: *adv.*, perhaps, albeit

licet, licere (2), licuit, licitum: (*impersonal verb*) be permitted

limen, liminis, n: door step

lingua, linguae, f: language

linteum, lintei, n: towel

litterae, litterarum, f: a letter

lixa, lixae, m: lictor (see 24n, line 477), attendant

locus, loci, m: room, space, place

locutor, locutoris, m: speaker

longe: *adv.*, long (time); far (space); *superlative* longissime.

loquax, loquacis: *adj.*, talkative

loquor, loqui, locutus sum: *vt.*, say, speak

lotium, lotii, n: urine, piss

lubricus, lubrica, lubricum: *adj.*, slippery, slick

lucerna, lucernae, f: lamp, light

lucidus, lucida, lucidum: *adj.*, bright, shining

Lucius, Lucii, m: name of main character of the novel

luctus, luctus, m: grieving

luna, lunae, f: moon

Lupus, Lupi, m: Mr. Wolf (see 5n, line 85)

luror, luroris, m: yellowness, pallor

lux, lucis, f: light, daylight

M

Macedonia, Macedoniae, f: Macedonia, region of northern Greece

macies, maciei, f: thinness, gauntness

mador, madoris, m: moisture

maeror, maeroris, m: weeping

magicus, magica, magicum: *adj.*, magical

magister, magistri, m: teacher

magisterium, magisterii, n: term of office, magistracy

magistratus, magistratus, m: magistracy, office

magnarius, magnaria, magnarium: *adj.*, big-time, wholesale

magnus, magna, magnum: *adj.*, large, great

malus, mala, malum: *adj.*, bad, evil, troublesome

mando (1): *vt.*, entrust

mane: *adv.*, in the morning

manes, manum, m: spirits of the dead

mansio, mansionis, f: place to stay, room, inn

mantica, manticae, f: satchel

manus, manus, f: hand

marcidus, marcida, marcidum: *adj.*, worn out

mare, maris, n: sea

margo, marginis, m: edge

mater, matris, f: mother

maternus, materna, maternum: *adj.*, of one's mother, maternal

matrimonium, matrimonii, n: marriage

maturius: *comparative adv.*, rather quickly

matutinus, matutina, matutinum: *adj.*, in the morning, morning's

maxime: *superlative adv.*, especially

meaculum, meaculi, n: passage

mecum = *cum me*

Medea, Medeae, f: Medea; see 10n, line 175

medicus, medici, m: doctor, physician

medius, media, medium: *adj.*, mid-, middle of

mel, mellis, n: honey

membrum, membri, n: limb

memini, meminisse, —: *vt.*, remember

memoro (1): *vt.*, tell, recount, recall

mendacium, mendacii, n: lie

mendicans, mendicantis, m: beggar

mens, mentis, f: mind, intention

mensa, mensae, f: table

mensis, mensis, m: month

mentio (4): *vi.*, lie

merces, mercis, f: payment; *pl.*, merchandise

mereo, merere (2), merui, meritum: *vi.*, earn, work, earn a wage, serve (*military*)

Meroë: name of one of the witches who persecute Aristomenes and Socrates; *Meroen, acc.* (see 7n, line 127)

merus, mera, merum: *adj.*, plain, unmixed

metuo, metuere, metui, metutum: *vt.*, fear (for)

metus, metus, m: fear

meus, mea, meum: *possessive adj.*, my

mi: *vocative* of *meus* (irreg.)

Milesius, Milesia, Milesium: *adj.*, Milesian

Milo, Milonis, m: Milo, the name of Lucius' host in Hypata

ministerium, ministerii, n: aid, support

minor (1): *vt.*, threaten

minus: *comparative adv.*, less; *also* = *non*

miror (1): *vt.*, marvel at, be amazed at, wonder at

mirus, mira, mirum: *adj.*, amazing, marvelous

misellus, misella, misellum: *adj.*, (diminutive of *miser*) poor little, unhappy, wretched

miser, misera, miserum: *adj.*, unhappy, wretched, sad

misericordia, misericordiae, f: pity

mitigo (1): *vt.*, soften, make tender, make mellow

modeste: *adv.*, politely

modico: *adv.*, "a little"

modicus, modica, modicum: *adj.*, small, little, moderate

modo: *adv.*, merely, only, just (*time*)

modum: *adv.*, only

modus, modi, m: sort, kind

mollities, mollitiei, f: softness

momentum, momenti, n: moment

mons, montis, m: mountain

monstratus, monstratus, m: gesture

mores, morum, m: character, habits

morior, mori, mortuus sum: *vi.*, die

mors, mortis, f: death

mortales, mortalium, m: mortals, humans

mortiferus, mortifera, mortiferum: *adj.*, fatal

mox: *adv.*, soon, presently

mucro, mucronis, m: point, tip

mulier, mulieris, f: woman

multus, multa, multum: *adj.*, much, many

munitus, munita, munitum: *adj.*, protected

mutilus, mutila, mutilum: *adj.*, broken, deformed

muto (1): *vt.*, change, transform

mutuo (1): *vt.*, lend, grant a loan

mutuus, mutua, mutuum: *adj.*, common, shared, mutual

N

nam: *conj.*, because, for, for instance

narro (1): *vt.*, tell a story, tell, explain

naturalis, naturalis, naturale: *adj.*, natural

naturalitus: *adv.*, in accordance with nature

natus, nata, natum: *adj.*, born

ne: *conj.*, that ... not, lest (introduces negative subjunctive clauses of purpose and indirect commands)

-ne: *enclitic particle* = ?

ne: *particle*, indeed

nebula, nebulae, f: cloud

nec, neque: *conj.*, and not, nor, neither; *as correlative*, nec ... nec *or* neque ... neque, neither ... nor

necdum: *adv.*, not yet

necessarius, necessarii, m: close relation

negotiator, negotiatoris, m: business-man

negotium, negotii, n: business

nepos, nepotis, m: nephew

neque = *nec*

nequeo, nequere (2), nequivi, —: be unable

nequicquam: *adv.*, in vain

nescio (4): *vt.*, not know

nexus, nexus, m: bond

nidor, nidoris, m: smell

nihil: *indeclinable noun*, nothing; *adv.*, not at all

Niloticus, Nilotica, Niloticum: *adj.*, from the Nile

nimis: *adv.*, very much (more: see 7n, line 130)

nimius, nimia, nimium: *adj.*, excessive, too much

nisi: *conj.*, unless, if ... not

noceo, nocere (2), nocui, nocitum: *vi.*, hurt

nocturnus, nocturna, nocturnum: *adj.*, of night

nodosus, nodosa, nodosum: *adj.*, knotty

nodus, nodi, m: knot

nomen, nominis, n: name

non: *adv.*, not

nosco, noscere, novi, notum: *vt.*, find out, get to know

noster, nostra, nostrum: *possessive adj.*, our

novitas, novitatis, f: novelty

novus, nova, novum: *adj.*, new, unusual; *superlative*, novissimus, most recent nox, noctis, f: night

noxa, noxae, f: injury, harm

nudus, nuda, nudum: *adj.*, naked, unarmed

nugae, nugarum, f: trifles

nugamenta, nugamentorum, n: trifles, trash, junk

nullus, nulla, nullum: *adj.*, no, not any

numen, numinis, n: spirit, power

numero (1): *vt.*, count

nummatus, nummata, nummatum: *adj.*, having money, rich

nummi, nummorum, m: money

nummuli, nummulorum, m: money, coins

nunc: *adv.*, now, at the present moment

nuptiae, nuptiarum, f: marriage, wedding

O

o: *interj.* (used with the vocative to emphasize direct address)

ob: *prep. + acc.*, because of

obditus, obdita, obditum: *adj.*, fastened

obeo, obire, obii, obitum: *vi.*, die; go to find

obliquus, obliqua, obliquum: *adj.*, slanting

oboediens, oboedientis: *adj.*, obedient to, obeying

obseptus, obsepta, obseptum: *adj.*, sewn shut

obsessus, obsessa, obsessum: *adj.*, besieged, beset

obsono (1): *vi.*, shop, buy food, buy fish

obstinatio, obstinationis, f: stubborness

obstino (1): *vt.*, resolve, determine, persist

obstupidus, obstupida, obstupidum: *adj.*, speechless

obtego, obtegere, obtexi, obtectum: *vt.*, cover

obtero, obterere, obtrivi, obtritum: *vt.*, grind down

obtutus, obtutus, m: gaze, look

occido, occidere, occisi, occisum: *vt.*, kill

occipitium, occipitii, n: the back of the head

ociter: *adv.*, quickly

octo: *indeclinable adj.*, eight

oculus, oculi, m: eye

odor, odoris, m: smell

offendo, offendere, offendi, offensum: *vi.*, offend, find, meet

offero, offerre, obtuli, oblatum: *vt.*, present, display

officialis, officialis, m: assistant, clerk

officiosus, officiosa, officiosum: *adj.*, dutiful

officium, officii, n: duty, function

offula, offulae, f: morsel

offulcio, offulcire, offulsi, offulsum: *vt.*, stanch, stop up, close

oleum, olei, n: oil

ominor (1): *vt.*, give an omen, suggest

omnino: *adv.*, at all

omnis, omnis, omne: each, every

omnividens, omnividentis: *adj.*, all-seeing

onus, oneris, n: burden

operose: *adv.*, vigorously

operulae, operularum, f: wages

opinio, opinionis, f: opinion

opiparis, opiparis, opipare: *adj.*, sumptuous

opperior, opperire, oppertus sum: *vt.*, wait (for), await

oppessulatus, oppessulata, oppessulatum: *adj.*, bolted

optatus, optata, optatum: *adj.*,
　longed-for, desirable
optime: *adv.*, best
optimus, optima, optimum:
　superlative adj., best, highest
opulentus, opulenta, opulentum:
　adj., rich
oriens, orientis: *adj.*, rising
origo, originis, f: origin, beginning
ornatus, ornata, ornatum: *adj.*,
　refined, distinguished
oro (1): *vi.*, pray; *as polite word*,
　please
os, oris, n: mouth
ostium, ostii, n: door

p

paene: *adv.*, almost, nearly
paenitet, paenitere (2), paenituit:
　regret (see 12n, line 229)
palaestrita, palaestritae, m:
　wrestling-coach
palam: *adv.*, openly
palliastrum, palliastri, n: cheap
　cloak
pallor, palloris, m: paleness
palpito (1): *vt.*, beat, drum, pound
palus, paludis, f: pool, pond, marsh
pan, panis, n: bread
Panthia, Panthiae f: name of one
　of the witches who torments
　Aristomenes (see 12n, line 220)
papyrus, papyri, f: papyrus
parco, parcere, peperci, —: spare,
　take it easy on; parce! *as an
　interjection*, stop! (see 2n, line 33)
parens, parentis, m/f: parent, father,
　mother
pareo, parere (2), parui, paritum:
　vi., appear
paries, parietis, m: wall
pario, parere, peperi, partum: *vt.*,
　give birth to, produce
paro (1): *vt.*, prepare, get ready, get

pars, partis, f: part, place, direction
parsimonia, parsimoniae, f:
　frugality
participo (1): *vt.*, share in
parvulus, parvula, parvulum: *adj.*,
　small, tiny
parvus, parva, parvum: *adj.*, small
pasco, pascere, pavi, pastum: *vt.*,
　feed, support
passim: *adv.*, here and there
patefacio, patefacere, patefeci,
　patefactum: *vt.*, expose, open
　up; *passive*, patefio
pateo, patere (2), patui, —: *vi.*, lie
　open, be exposed
pater, patris, m: father
patior, pati, passus sum: *vt.*, allow
pator, patoris, m: opening, hollow
patria, patriae, f: homeland,
　country, fatherland
pauca: *adv.* (= *pauca verba*), briefly
pauci, paucae, pauca: *adj.*, few, a
　few
paulo: *adv.*, (by) a little
paululum: *adv.*, a little
pauperies, pauperiei, f: poverty
pavor, pavoris, m: fear, dread
pectus, pectoris, n: heart, chest,
　breast
penitus: *adv.*, deeply, deep within
per: *prep.* + *acc.*, through, along, by
　way of, by
peralbus, peralba, peralbum: *adj.*,
　quite white
percitus, percita, percitum: *adj.*,
　aroused
percontor (1): *vt.*, ask, inquire, find
　out
percrebro, percrebrere, percrebrui,
　—: *vi.*, grow widespread,
　escalate
percussus, percussa, percussum:
　adj., stunned
perdo, perdere, perdidi, perditum:
　vt., destroy, ruin

perduco, perducere, perduxi, perductum: *vt.*, take, bring, lead to

peregrinatio, peregrinationis, f: journey

peregrinor (1): *vi.*, travel abroad, live abroad

peremo, peremere, peremi, peremptum: *vt.*, do in, detsroy

perfluo, perfluere, perfluxi, perfluxum: *vi.*, flow through, run through, stream

perforor (1): *vt.*, poke holes in

perfringo, perfringere, perfregi, perfractum: *vt.*, break open, undo

perfundo, perfundere, perfudi, perfusum: *vt.*, pour over, soak, suffuse

pergo, pergere, perrexi, perrectum: *vi.*, continue, keep on

perhibeo, perhibere (2), perhibui, perhibitum: *vt.*, hold to be, regard as, allege, say

perluo, perluere, perlui, perlutum: *vt.*, soak

permulceo, permulcere (2), permulsi, permulsum: *vt.*, soothe, stroke, caress

perpessus: *ppp.* < perpetior, perpeti, perpessus sum: *vt.*, endure

perpetro (1): *vt.*, carry out, commit

perpetuus, perpetua, perpetuum: *adj.*, unending, eternal

persolvo, persolvere, persolvi, persolutum: *vt.*, perform, complete, pay

pertentatus, pertentata, pertentatum: *adj.*, overextended, taxed

pertexo, pertexere, pertexui, pertextum: *vt.*, tell, weave together

perveho, pervehere, pervexi, pervectum: *vt.*, carry, transport

pervenio, pervenire, perveni, perventum: *vi.*, arrive

pes, pedis, m: foot, leg (of a bed)

pessulus, pessuli, m: bolt

pestilens, pestilentis: *adj.*, noxious, malignant

peto, petere, petivi, petitum: *vt.*, ask, go for, head for

philosophus, philosophi, m: philosopher

piger, pigra, pigrum: *adj.*, slow, dull, inactive

piget, pigere (2), pigui, —: *vt.*, disgust (see 3n, line 46)

pignus, pignoris, n: security, collateral

piscator, piscatoris, m: fisherman

piscatus, piscatus, m: fishing, a catch of fish

piscis, piscis, m: fish

placidus, placida, placidum: *adj.*, peaceful, quiet

plane: *adv.*, clearly, certainly, of course

planus, plana, planum: *adj.*, flat, plain, clear

platanus, platani, f: plane tree

plures, plures, plura: *adj.*, more

plurimus, plurima, plurimum: *superlative adj.*, the most, very many

Plutarchus, Plutarchi, m: Plutarch (see 2n, line 19)

poculum, poculi, n: cup

poecilen: *Greek acc., adj., singular f:* painted

pol: *interj.*, by Pollux

polenta, polentae, f: barley-porridge

pollex, pollicis, m: thumb

polliceor, polliceri, pollicitus sum: *vt.*, promise

pomerium, pomerii, n: the city border

pondus, ponderis, n: weight

pone: *prep. + acc.*, behind

pono, ponere, posui, positum: *vt.*, lay, put out

populus, populi, m: people, the people

porrigo, porrigere, porrexi, porrectum: *vt.*, stretch forward, extend

porro: *adv.*, besides, moreover

porta, portae, f: gate

porticus, porticus, f: porch

possum, posse, potui, — : *vi.*, be able

post: *prep. + acc.*, after

postis, postis, m: door-post

postliminio: *adv.*, back

postquam: *conj.*, after

postremum: *adv.*, last of all

postumus, postumi, m: a child born after the death of the father

pote: *adv.*, (with *quam*) rather ... (than)

potens, potentis: *adj.*, powerful, able (+ inf.)

potius: *adv.*, rather, instead

prae: *prep. + abl.*, because of, in the face of

praeacutus, praeacuta, praeacutum: *adj.*, sharpened

praecedens, praecedentis: *adj.*, past, former

praecipuus, praecipua, praecipuum: *adj.*, important

praecisio, praecisionis, f: chewing off

praeeo, praeire, praeii, praeitum: *vi.*, supervise, lead the way

praefero, praeferre, praetuli, praelatum: *vt.*, value ... ahead of, prefer

praefor (1): *vt.*, beg for in advance

praegnatio, praegnationis, f: pregnancy

praeministro (1): *vt.*, do (as a service) before (being asked)

praesecatus, praesecata, praesecatum: *adj.*, severed, cut through

praeses, praesidis, m: one in charge, governor

praesidium, praesidii, n: protection, refuge

praestino (1): *vt.*, buy

praeter: *prep. + acc.*, except for

praeterea: *conj.*, besides

praetereo, praeterire, praeterii, praeteritum: *vt.*, pass by

prandium, prandii, n: lunch, meal

pratum, prati, n: meadow

pravus, prava, pravum: *adj.*, degenerate

pretium, pretii, n: price

pridie: *adv.*, the day before

primores, primorium, m: leading citizens

primus, prima, primum: *adj.*, first, earliest; *adv.* (*primum*), first

prior, prior, prius: *comparative adj.*, earlier, first

pristinus, pristina, pristinum: *adj.*, former

prius: *adv.*, earlier, first, before; *conj., with quam*, before

privo (1): deprive, take away

pro: *prep. + abl.*, for, on behalf of, in front of, in proportion to

probe: *adv.*, well, thoroughly, properly

probrum, probri, n: disgrace, reproach

probus, proba, probum: *adj.*, excellent, honest

procedo, procedere, processi, processum: *vi.*, go forward, come forward, walk ahead

proclamo (1): *vi.*, shout out

proclivis, proclivis, proclive: *adj.*, inclined, prone, eager

procuro (1): take care of, see to

prodeo, prodire, prodii, proditum: *vi.*, issue forth, result

proditus, prodita, proditum: *adj.*, endowed, equipped

produco, producere, produxi, productum: *vt.*, lead, take

profecto: *adv.*, after all, to be sure

profero, proferre, protuli, prolatum: *vt.*, bring out, provide; explain, answer, report

proficiscor, proficisci, profectus sum: *vi.*, set out go forth, leave

profundo, profundere, profudi, profusum: *vt.*, pour

profundus, profunda, profundum: *adj.*, deep

progredior, progredi, progressus sum: *vi.*, go forward, walk forward

proicio, proicere, proieci, proiectum: *vt.*, throw forward, throw out

prolixus, prolixa, prolixum: *adj.*, lengthy

promineo, prominere (2), prominui, —: *vi.*, stick out

promptuarium, promptuarii, n: store-room

pronuntio (1): declare

pronus, prona, pronum: *adj.*, face down

propere: *adv.*, quickly

properiter: *adv.*, quickly

propitiatus, propitiata, propitiatum: *adj.*, appeased, reconciled

propius: *comparative adv.*, closer

propter: *prep. + acc.*, because of

prorsus: *adv.*, utterly, wholly

prosapia, prosapiae, f: lineage, stock

prospicio, prospicere, prospexi, prospectum: *vt.*, look out over, seek out, find

prospicue: *adv.*, thoughtfully, providently

prosterno, prosternere, prostravi, prostratum: *vt.*, lay flat, flatten

proveho, provehere, provexi, provectum: *vt.*, carry forward, advance

provenio, provenire, proveni, proventum: *vi.*, turn out, happen

provincialis, provincialis, provinciale: *adj.*, of the province, provincial

proxime: *adv.*, closest, most closely

proximum: *adv.*, closest, most closely

proximus, proxima, proximum: *superlative adj.*, closest, nearest

prudens, prudentis: *adj.*, wise, judicious

pubes, pubis, f: groin

publicitus: *adv.*, in public

pudor, pudoris, m: shame, modesty

puer, pueri, m: boy

pueritia, pueritiae, f: boyhood

pulso (1): *vt.*, knock, beat

punicans, punicantis: *adj.*, red, blushing

puto (1): think, judge

putris, putris, putre: *adj.*, rotten

Pythias, Pythiae, m: Pythias, the name of the Aedile in our story (see 24n, line 470)

Q

qua: *adv.*, where

quaestio, quaestionis, f: question, inquiry

quaestus, quaestus, m: trade, business
qualia, *adj.,* just like
quam: *adv.,* how, to what extent; *with superlative adj.'s and adv.'s,* as ... as possible; *with comparative adj.'s and adv.'s,* than; *conj.* (with *prius*), before; *correlatively with tam,* as
quamquam: *conj.,* although
quamvis: *adv.,* no matter how ...
quanti: *genitive of value,* for how much?
quasi: *conj.,* as if; *adv.,* so to speak, as it were, nearly
quatior, quati, quassus sum: *vi.,* shake, tremble
quemadmodum = quem ad modum, *adv.,* in what way, how
queo, quere (2), quivi, —: *vi.,* be able
qui, quae, quod: *relative pron.,* who, which; *relative adj.,* which, and this; *as exclamatory adj.,* what a ...!
quidam, quaedam, quoddam: *indef. adj.,* a certain, some, a
quidem: *adv.,* indeed, especially
quies, quietis, f: rest
quiesco, quiescere, quievi, quietum: *vi.,* rest
quietus, quieta, quietum: *adj.,* peaceful, restful
quin: *conj.,* why ... not
quippe: *conj.,* inasmuch as
Quirites, Quiritium, m: Romans, Roman citizens
quis, quid: *interrogative pron.,* who, what
quisquiliae, quisquiliarum, f: rubbish, trash
quoad, *conj.,* until (*with subjunctive*); to the point where (*with indicative*)
quod: *conj.,* because

quoniam: *conj.,* since, because
quoque: *adv.,* also

R

radix, radicis, f: root
ramulus, ramuli, m: branch
rana, ranae, m: frog
rancidus, rancida, rancidum: *adj.,* foul, disgusting, stinking
rapio, rapere, rapui, raptum: *vt.,* steal
ratiocinor (1): *vt.,* ponder, reflect on, calculate
raucus, rauca, raucum: *adj.,* hoarse
reapse: *adv.,* in reality
reatus, reatus, m: trial, defense
rebullio (4): *vt.,* bubble back, keep bubbling
recens, recentis: *adj.,* fresh, new; *recens* as *adv.,* newly
receptaculum, receptaculi, n: shelter
recido, recidere, reccidi, recasum: *vi.,* fall back
recipio, recipere, recepi, receptum: *vt.,* take ... back
reciprocus, reciproca, reciprocum: *adj.,* changeable
recordor (1): recall
recte: *adv.,* correctly, rightly
recurro, recurrere, recurri, recursum: *vi.,* run back, return
reddo, reddere, reddidi, redditum: *vt.,* bring, bring back
redeo, redire, redii, reditum: *vi.,* go back, return
reduco, reducere, reduxi, reductum: *vt.,* draw back, lead back, slide back (bolts)
refero, referre, rettuli, relatum: *vt.,* report, bring back; *reflexive,* return

reficio, reficere, refeci, refectum: *vt.*, refresh, restore

refoveo, refovere (2), refovi, refotum: *vt.*, restore, refresh

regina, reginae, f: queen

regio, regionis, f: territory, area, region

regredior, regredi, regressus sum: *vi.*, go back, step back

religio, religionis, f: ritual

relinquo, relinquere, reliqui, relictum: *vt.*, leave behind, abandon

reliquus, reliqua, reliquum: *adj.*, remaining

remeo (1): *vi.*, come back (up)

remetior (4): *vt.*, go over again

removeo, removere (2), removi, remotum: *vt.*, remove, take away

remulceo, remulcere (2), remulsi, remulsum: *vt.*, stroke

renitor, reniti, renisus sum: *vt.*, resist

renudo (1): *vt.*, reveal, lay bare

repagulum, repaguli, n: bar

repello, repellere, reppuli, repulsum: *vt.*, push away

repente: *adv.*, suddenly

repigratus, repigrata, repigratum: *adj.*, held back, held within

replaudo, replaudere, replausi, replausum: *vt.*, smack repeatedly

replico (1): *vt.*, turn over, think (*with mecum*)

repono, reponere, reposui, repositum: *vt.*, put back, return

reporto, reportare, reportavi, reportatum: *used reflexively*, return, go back

res, rei, f: thing, property, situation, factor (supply best meaning from context)

resero (1): *vt.*, unbolt, open

reservo (1): *vt.*, keep back, save

resideo, residere (2), resedi, resessum: *vi.*, be seated, sit back (in the original position)

resido, residere, resedi, resessum: *vi.*, sit back (in), squat

resisto, resistere, restiti, —: *vi.*, resist

respicio, respicere, respexi, respectum: *vt.*, look back at

respondeo, respondere (2), respondi, responsum: *vt.*, answer, reply; resemble (= *correspondere*, see 1n, line 16)

respuo, respuere, respui, —: *vt.*, reject, spurn

restis, restis, f: rope

resurgo, resurgere, resurrexi, resurrectum: *vi.*, return, go back up

retineo, retinere (2), retinui, retentum: *vt.*, hold back, keep hold of

revortor, revorti, reversus sum: *vi.*, go back, return, turn back

ripa, ripae, f: bank (of a river)

risus, risus, m: laugh

rogo (1): *vt.*, ask, ask for

roncus, ronci, m: croak

ros, roris, m: moisture, dew

roscidus, roscida, roscidum: *adj.*, wet, moist, dewy

rudis, rudis, rude: *adj.*, uneducated, unpolished, new, unusual

rursum: *adv.*, back, again

S

saccaria, saccariae, f: the job of a porter

saepicule: *adv.*, rather often

saevio (4): *vi.*, rage

saevitia, saevitiae, f: viciousness, cruelty

saevus, saeva, saevum: *adj.*, savage, vicious

saga, sagae, f: witch

salebra, salebrorum, n: uneven roads, rough roads

saltatio, saltationis, f: dance

saltem: *adv.*, at least, to be sure

salto (1): *vt.*, dance, hop upon

salutaris, salutaris, salutare: *adj.*, saving, rescuing

salve: *adv.*, well, happily

sanctissime: *superlative adv.*, most solemnly

sanguis, sanguinis, m: blood

sanus, sana, sanum: *adj.*, healthy

sapor, saporis, m: taste

sarcina, sarcinae, f: bag, pack, load

sarcinula, sarcinulae, f: (small) bag, bundle

sat: *adv.*, enough, quite, very

satis: *adv.*, enough, sufficiently; very

saxum, saxi, n: rock

scaenicus, scaenica, scaenicum: *adj.*, of the stage, dramatic

scelus, sceleris, n: crime

scientia, scientiae, f: expertise, science, practice

scilicet: *adv.*, without doubt, to be sure (indicates sarcasm or irony)

scio, scire, scivi, scitum: *vt.*, know

scissilus, scissila, scissilum: *adj.*, torn

scitulus = *scitus*

scitus, scita, scitum: *adj.*, nice, sharp, clever

scopulus, scopuli, m: cliff, crag

scorteus, scortea, scorteum: *adj.*, leathery

scortum, scorti, n: whore

scribo, scribere, scripsi, scriptum: *vt.*, write

scrobis, scrobis, m: ditch

scrupulosissime: *superlative adv.*, in great detail, on every single point

scrupulus, scrupuli, m: gravel, a small weight, cause for concern

scrutor (1): probe

secundum: *prep. + acc.*, according to, after

secus: *adv.*, apart; *often with* modico, a little apart, unusually

sed: *conj.*, but, but rather

sedentarius, sedentaria, sedentarium: *adj.*, resulting from sitting

sedeo, sedere (2), sedi, sessum: *vi.*, sit

sedulo: *adv.*, assiduously, constantly

semiamictus, semiamicta, semiamictum: *adj.*, half-clothed

semiamputatus, semiamputata, semiamputatum: *adj.*, half cut off

semimortuus, semimortua, semimortuum: *adj.*, half dead

semisomnus, semisomna, semisomnum: *adj.*, half asleep

semisopitus, semisopita, semisopitum: *adj.*, half asleep

semper: *adv.*, always, forever

sempiterna: *adv.*, forever

senex, senis, m: old man

seniculus, seniculi, m: (little) old man

sensim: *adv.*, gradually, slowly

sentio, sentire, sensi, sensum: *vt.*, feel, perceive, understand, realize

sepelio (4): *vt.*, bury

sepulcralis, sepulcralis, sepulcrale: *adj.*, funereal, burial

sequor, sequi, secutus sum: *vt.*, follow

series, seriei, f: succession, series

sermo, sermonis, m: conversation, speech, language

sero: *adv.*, later, late, recently

serpens, serpentis, m: snake

servitus, servitutis, f: slavery

sessibulum, sessibuli, n: seat

severissime: *superlative adv.*, very harshly

severitudo, severitudinis, f: harshness, strictness, severity

Sextus, Sexti, m: name of Plutarch's nephew (see 2n, line 19)

si: *conj.*, if

sic: *adv.*, thus, so, in this way

sidus, sideris, n: star, constellation

sileo, silere (2), silui, —: *vi.*, be silent

similis, similis, simile: *adj.*, like, similar to

similiter: *adv.*, in a similar way

simul: *adv.*, together, at the same time

simulacrum, simulacri, n: shape, image, apparition

sine: *imper.* (< sino), let (it) go, stop (see 7n, line 108)

sine: *prep. + abl.*, without

singula, singulorum, n: one thing at a time, individual answers

sinister, sinistra, sinistrum: *adj.*, left

siparium, siparii, n: backdrop, curtain

siquis, siquid: = *si (ali)quis, si (ali)quid*, if anyone, if anything, if ... at all

sitio (4): *vi.*, be thirsty

sititor, sititoris, m: one who thirsts, a thirsty person

situs, sita, situm: *adj.*, located

Socrates: name of Aristomenes' friend cursed by witches; Socraten, *acc.*

sodes: *interj.* (= *si audes*), please

sol, solis, m: sun

soleo, solere (2), solui, solitum: *vi.*, be accustomed

solitudo, solitudinis, f: wasteland, wilderness

solitus, solita, solitum: *adj (ppp. < solere)*, usual, ordinary

sollertia, sollertiae, f: cleverness

sollicitudo, sollicitudinis, f: anxiety, worry

solum, soli, n: ground, soil

solus, sola, solum: *adj.*, alone, only; *adv.*, only

somnio (1): *vi.*, dream

somnium, somnii, n: dream

somnolentus, somnolenta, somnolentum: *adj.*, sleepy

somnus, somni, m: sleep

sopitus, sopita, sopitum: *adj.*, drowsy

sordes, sordis, f: dirt, filth, stinginess

soror, sororis, f: sister

Spartiacus, Spartiaca, Spartiacum: *adj.*, near Sparta, Spartan

spatha, spathae, f: broad bladed sword

species, speciei, f: shape, form; category (see 22n, line 421)

specimen, speciminis, n: example

speciosus, speciosa, speciosum: *adj.*, attractive, comely, seemly

spectaculum, spectaculi, n: show

sperno, spernere, sprevi, spretum: *vt.*, shrink from, refuse, reject

spes, spei, f: hope

spiritus, spiritus, m: breath, spirit

spoliatio, spoliationis, f: robbery

spongia, spongiae, f: sponge

sponte: *adv.*, freely, willingly

sportula, sportulae, f: little basket

spurcus, spurca, spurcum: *adj.*, filthy

stabularius, stabularii, m: inn-keeper

stabulum, stabuli, n: stopping–place, inn

statim: *adv.*, immediately

statuo, statuere, statui, statutum: *vi.*, decide

status, status, m: condition

stella, stellae, f: star

sterilis, sterilis, sterile: *adj.*, infertile, barren

sterto, stertere, stertui, —: *vi.*, snore

stilla, stillae, f: drop

stilus, stili, m: stylus, pen

stipendium, stipendii, n: tour of duty

stipes, stipis, f: donation

stirps, stirpis, f: lineage

strenue: *adv.*, energetically, working hard

stridor, stridoris, m: screech

studium, studii, n: eagerness, pursuit, zeal; *pl.*, studies

stupor, stuporis, m: stunned silence

suadeo, suadere (2), suasi, suasum: *vi.*, persuade, urge

sub: *prep. + abl.*, under

subcubans, subcubantis: *adj.*, lying underneath

subditus, subdita, subditum: *adj.*, flush, fitting from the bottom

subeo, subire, subii, subitum: *vi.*, go up from under

subicio, subicere, subieci, subiectum: *vt.*, put in, interject

subinde: *adv.*, repeatedly

sublimo (1): *vt.*, raise to heaven

submissus, submissa, submissum: *adj.*, sunken, submerged

subrideo, subridere (2), subrisi, subrisum: *vi.*, smile quietly, chuckle

subsidium, subsidii, n: help, aid

subterhabeo, subterhabere (2), subterhabui, subterhabitum: *vt.*, give a low value to, disdain

succussus, succussus, m: shaking

succutio, succutere, succussi, succussum: *vt.*, shake up

sudor, sudoris, m: sweat

sufficiens, sufficientis: *adj.*, adequate

sufficit, sufficere, suffecit, suffectum: *vi.*, it is enough

sum, esse, fui, —: *vi.*, be

summe: *adv.*, mostly, mainly, especially

sumministro (1): *vt.*, supply, provide

summus, summa, summum: *superlative adj.*, highest, greatest, top of

sumo, sumere, sumpsi, sumptum: *vt.*, pick up, take up, take (for eating)

supellex, supellectilis, f: furniture

super: *prep. + acc.*, over, above

superior, superior, superius: *comparative adj.*, higher

superruo, superruere, superrui, superrutum: *vt.*, ovewhelm, rush over

supersum, superesse, superfui, —: *vi.*, survive, live

supervivens, superviventis: *adj.*, surviving

suppetior (1): *vi.*, bring help

suppositus, supposita, suppositum: *adj.*, shoved up, wedged

supra: *prep. + acc.*, above

sursum: *adv.*, up, upwards

suscipio, suscipere, suscepi, susceptum: *vt.*, pick up

suspendeo, suspendere (2),
suspendi, suspensum: *vt.*, hang
up, raise

suspiritus, suspiritus, m: sigh

sustineo, sustinere (2), sustinui,
sustentum: *vt.*, hold ... up, put
up with, endure

susurramen, susurraminis, n:
incantation

susurrus, susurri, m: murmur,
whisper

sutilis, sutilis, sutile: *adj.*,
stitched

t

taceo, tacere (2), tacui, tacitum: *vi.*,
be quiet

tacitus, tacita, tacitum: *adj.*, silent

taedet, taedere (2), taeduit, —: *vt.*,
bore (see 3n, line 46)

taedium, taedii, n: boredom

Taenaros: (*nominative*) Mt.
Taenaros, in the Peloponnesus

talis, talis, tale: *adj.*, of such a sort,
such

tam: *intensive adv.*, to such an
extent, so; *correlative in tam ...*
quam, as ... as.

tamen, *conj.*, nevertheless, however

tandem: *adv.*, finally, at last

tantus, tanta, tantum: *adj.*, so
much, so great, so big, this
much

Tartara, Tartarorum, n: Tartarus,
the depths of the underworld

tego, tegere, texi, tectum: *vt.*, hide,
cover, protect

telum, teli, n: weapon

temero (1): *vt.*, make a rash advance
on

tempero (1): *vi.*, restrain

tempus, temporis, n: time; *pro*
tempore, for a while; *ex tempore,*
on the spur of the moment

temulentus, temulenta,
temulentum: *adj.*, a little tipsy,
a bit drunk

teneo, tenere (2), tenui, tentum:
vt., support, drag out

tenuis, tenuis, tenue: *adj.*, slender,
meager

tenus: *postpositive prep. + abl.*, up
to

terra, terrae, f: earth, ground

tersus, tersus, m: wiping

tertius, tertia, tertium: *adj.*, third

testis, testis, m: witness

testudo, testudinis, f: turtle

Theseus, Thesei, m: name of
Lucius' father

Thessalia, Thessaliae, f:
Thessaly, region in northeast
Greece

Thessalicus, Thessalica,
Thessalicum: *adj.*, Thessalian

tigillum, tigilli, n: little beam

titubo (1): *vi.*, wobble, stagger, reel

tollo, tollere, sustuli, sublatus: *vt.*,
remove

tortuosus, tortuosa, tortuosum:
adj., twisted

tot: *indeclinable adj.*, so many

totus, tota, totum: *adj.*, the whole,
all

tracto (1): treat, handle

trado, tradere, tradidi, traditum:
vt., hand over

tragicus, tragica, tragicum: *adj.*,
tragic

traho, trahere, traxi, tractum: *vt.*,
drag, pull

transeo, transire, transii,
transitum: *vt.*, go past, go
across

transfero, transferre,
transtuli, translatum: *vt.*,
transport

transitus, transitus, m: way past

tremor, tremoris, m: trembling

trepidus, trepida, trepidum: *adj.*, trembling, fearful

triviae, triviarum, f: crossroads, side-streets

tropaeum, tropaei, n: trophy

trux, trucis: *adj.*, fierce, ferocious, savage

tumultuarius, tumultuaria, tumultuarium: *adj.*, hastily-contrived, chaotic

tunc: *adv.*, then, at that time

turbo (1): disrupt, alter, change

tutamentum, tutamenti, n: safe opportunity

tutor, tutoris, m: guardian

tuus, tua, tuum: *possessive adj.*, your

U

ubi: *conj.*, where, when

ubique: *adv.*, everywhere

Ulixes, Ulixis, m: Ulysses, Odysseus

ullus, ulla, ullum: *adj.*, any

ulterius: *adv.*, farther

ultime: *adv.*, farthest

ultro: *adv.*, on the other side

ultroneus, ultronea, ultroneum: *adj.*, voluntary

umbilicus, umbilici, m: navel

una: *adv.*, together

unctus, unctus, m: rubbing (oil)

unde: *interrog. adv.*, from where

unicus, unica, unicum: *adj.*, a single, one

unus, una, unum: *adj.*, one

urbs, urbis, f: city

urigo, uriginis, f: lust

urina, urinae, f: urine, piss

usquam: *adv.*, anywhere

usque: *adv.*, up to

usus, usus, m: use, experience

ut: *conj., with indicative*, when, as; *with subjunctive*, so that, in order that, that; *in similes*, just as.

utcumque: *adv.*, howsoever

uterque, utraque, utrumque: *adj.*, both, each

uterus, uteri, m: womb

utique: *adv.*, by all means, certainly

utor, uti, usus sum: *vi.*, use, employ

utpote: *conj.*, inasmuch as

utriculus, utriculi, m: little leather jug

uxor, uxoris, f: wife

V

vacuus, vacua, vacuum: *adj.*, empty

validus, valida, validum: *adj.*, strong, vigorous

valles, vallis, f: valley, vale

valva, valvae, f: panel, leaf (of a door)

varicus: *adv.*, with legs spread

varius, varia, varium: *adj.*, different kinds of

vastus, vasta, vastum: *adj.*, boundless, gigantic

vector, vectoris, m: carrier (i.e., horse)

vegetatio, vegetationis, f: invigoration

vegetus, vegeta, vegetum: *adj.*, vigorous, lively

vehementer: *adv.*, strongly, vigorously, violently

veho, vehere, vexi, vectum: *vi.*, ride

vel: *conj.*, or; *used correlaltively* vel ... vel, either ... or; *adv.*, even (see 14n, line 265)

velatus, velata, velatum: *adj.*, covered, hidden

velut: *conj.*, just as

venatorius, venatoria, venatorium: *adj.*, hunting, for the hunt

venerius, veneria, venerium: *adj.*, sexual

venia, veniae, f: pardon

venio, venire, veni, ventum: *vi.*, come

ventus, venti, m: wind

Venus, Veneris, f: Venus, goddess of love; *used by metonymy* = sex

verbero (1): *vt.*, beat

verbum, verbi, n: word, speech; *in the idiom,* in verba, see 2n, line 33

vere: *adv.*, truly

verecundia, verecundiae, f: modesty, good manners

vereor, vereri, veritus sum: *vt.*, fear

vernaculus, vernaculi, m: family slave

vero: *adv.*, truly, indeed, really

vertex, verticis, m: top

verum: *adv.*, but, but rather

verus, vera, verum: *adj.*, true, real

vesanus, vesani, m: fool, idiot, madman

vesica, vesicae, f: bladder

vespera: *adv.*, in the evening

vesperi: *adv.*, in the evening

vestigium, vestigii, n: step, pace

vestio (4): *vt.*, clothe

vetus, veteris: *adj.*, old, long-standing

vexatio, vexationis, f: discomfort

via, viae, f: road, street

viator, viatoris, m: traveler

vice, f: *abl. of* vicis (*no gen.*), lot, fortune

vicinia, viciniae, f: neighborhood

vicinus, vicina, vicinum: *adj.*, neighboring, nearby

vicissitudo, vicissitudinis, f: change, alteration

victima, victimae, f: sacrificial victim

video, videre (2), vidi, visum: *vt.*, see; *in passive, vi.*, seem

vigilia, vigiliae, f: watch (time of night: 11n, line 205)

vigilo (1): *vi.*, stay awake, remain alert

viginti: *indeclinable adj.*, twenty

villula, villulae, f: (small) country house, (small) estate

vindico (1): punish

vinolentia, vinolentiae, f: wine-drinking

vinum, vini, n: wine

violentia, violentiae, f: force, violence

vir, viri, m: man

virga, virgae, f: rod, staff (carried by a lictor, see 24n, line 477, on *lixas*)

virginalis, virginalis, virginale: *adj.*, maidenly

virilia, virilium, n: genitals

virtus, virtutis, f: virtue, excellence

viscera, viscerum, n: insides

viso, visere, visi, —: *vt.*, see, visit

visu: *supine* (< video), *abl. of respect*, seeing, to see

vitalis, vitalis, vitale: *adj.*, life-sustaining

vitrum, vitri, n: glass

vix: *adv.*, scarcely, with difficulty

vocaliter: *adv.*, in a loud voice

voco (1): *vt.*, call

volo, velle, volui, — : *vi.*, wish, want

voluptas, voluptatis, f: pleasure

votum, voti, n: prayer, vow

vox, vocis, f: language, voice, sound

vulnus, vulneris, n: wound

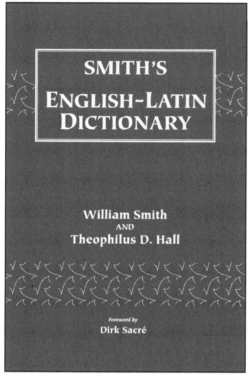

Variety Intermediate/Advanced Latin

ℬ LATIN Readers

Series Editor: Ronnie Ancona

These readers, written by experts in the field, provide well annotated Latin selections to be used as authoritative introductions to Latin authors, genres, or topics, for intermediate or advanced college Latin study. Their relatively small size (covering 500–600 lines) makes them ideal to use in combination. Each volume includes a comprehensive introduction, bibliography for further reading, Latin text with notes at the back, and complete vocabulary. Sixteen volumes (below) are scheduled for publication; others are under consideration. Check our website for updates: www.BOLCHAZY.com.

A Lucan Reader
Selections from CIVIL WAR
Susanna Braund

xxxiv + 134 pp. (2009) 5" x 7¾" Paperback ISBN 978-0-86516-661-5

Lucan's epic poem, *Civil War*, portrays the stark, dark horror of the years 49 through 48 BCE, the grim reality of Romans fighting Romans, of Julius Caesar vs. Pompey the Great. The introduction to this volume situates Lucan as a poet closely connected with the Stoics at Rome, working during the reign of the emperor Nero, in the genre inherited from Virgil.

The selections are intended for third- and fourth-year college curricula, and include Lucan's analysis of the causes of the civil war, depictions of his protagonists Caesar and Pompey at key moments—Caesar's crossing of the Rubicon, the assassination of Pompey as he arrives in Egypt seeking refuge, Cato's funeral oration for Pompey, Caesar's visit to the site of Troy—as well as highly atmospheric passages: Pompey's vision of his dead wife, Julia; and the necromancy performed by the witch Erichtho for Pompey's son.

Notes to the passages illuminate Lucan's attitude towards his material—his reluctance to tackle the topic of civil war, his complicated relationship with Virgil's *Aeneid*, and his passionate involvement in the events through the rhetorical device of apostrophe, when he seems to enter the poem as a character himself.

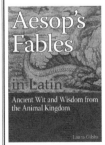

Aesop's Fables in Latin
Ancient Wit and Wisdom from the Animal Kingdom
Laura Gibbs

xxv + 356 pp. (2009) 7" x 10" Paperback ISBN 978-0-86516-695-0

This intermediate Latin reader allows students to review grammar and syntax and increase their knowledge of Latin prose style while they read eighty Aesop's fables in Latin prose, taken from the seventeenth-century edition illustrated by Francis Barlow. These Latin prose fables are ideal for Latin language students: simple, short, witty, and to-the-point, with a memorable moral lesson that provides a jumping-off point for discussion. Forty original black-and-white Barlow illustrations and 129 pertinent Latin proverbs are featured, spurs for classroom discussion. Selected fables include many that have become proverbial, such as "The Tortoise and The Hare" and "The Dog in the Manger," along with lesser known fables.

This is the perfect ancillary for intermediate students, to increase comprehension, confidence, and enthusiasm for reading Latin.

 Bolchazy-Carducci Publishers, Inc.
1570 Baskin Road
Mundelein, IL 60060
Phone: (847) 526-4344
www.bolchazy.com

Superlative Advanced Latin Texts

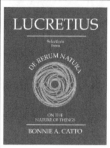

Lucretius
Selections from De rerum natura
Bonnie A. Catto

304 pp. (1998) 8 ½" x 11" Paperback ISBN 978-0-86516-399-7

The text includes 53 passages (1291 lines total) spanning the entire epic. Each section features a short introduction, discussion questions, vocabulary and extensive line-by-line notes on facing pages, and a wide variety of illustrative quotations from ancient as well as modern authors. Comprehensive vocabulary list at the back of the book.

Features: • Introduction • Latin text with short English introduction • Extensive facing-page notes • Discussion questions • Pertinent quotations from ancient and modern authors • Select bibliography • Complete vocabulary

"Those who wish to give second and third-year college students of Latin a good sampling of the *De rerum natura*, would do well to give this text their consideration." Following in the tradition of other learning texts offered by Bolchazy-Carducci, Catto's book offers the student not only a full sampling of the poem, but also an abundance of notes, vocabulary, and, perhaps most noteworthy of all, a *florilegium* of relevant passages selected from 'classical' and non-classical authors that bear upon the particular Lucretian passages to which they are attached."
> – C. A. Hoffman, *Bryn Mawr Classical Review*

"I wish more ancient authors were so splendidly served."
> – Richard F. Moorton, Jr., *New England Classical Journal*

Petronius
Selections from the Satyricon
Gilbert Lawall

vi + 66 pp. (1988) 6" x 9" Paperback ISBN 978-0-86516-288-4

Highly entertaining episodes selected from *Satyricon* and a student-friendly format make this book a bestseller.

Features: • Introduction • Selected Latin text (with macrons) from the *Satyricon*, including "A Scene at the Marketplace," "Trimachio's Dinner," "The Matron of Ephesus," "The Death of Lichas," and "Eating Human Flesh for Money" • Facing-page vocabulary • Same-page commentary • Appendix of Language and Style • Vocabulary

Lawall's *Petronius* is a *rara avis* indeed. His edition is one of the few, real Latin texts that a relative beginner to Latin can both manage and enjoy. As early as the second quarter of Latin I have introduced the class to Petronius. Inevitably the reaction has been enthusiastic. Would that there were similar editions of other Latin authors! With Petronius the teacher has no difficulty convincing students that studying Latin is worthwhile.
> – Sheila K. Dickison, University of Florida

". . . a class equipped with this book will find Petronius instructive and entertaining."
> – Ian Pratt, *JACT*

Bolchazy-Carducci Publishers, Inc.

1570 Baskin Road
Mundelein, IL 60060
Phone: (847) 526-4344
www.bolchazy.com

Made in the USA
San Bernardino, CA
30 March 2015